WATER GYPSIES

WATER GYPSIES

A HISTORY OF LIFE ON BRITAIN'S
RIVERS AND CANALS

JULIAN DUTTON
FOREWORD BY SAMUEL WEST

The
History
Press

First published 2021

The History Press
97 St George's Place, Cheltenham,
Gloucestershire, GL50 3QB
www.thehistorypress.co.uk

British Library Cataloguing in Publication Data.
A catalogue record for this book is available from the British Library.

ISBN 978 0 7509 9559 7

Typesetting and origination by The History Press
Printed in Turkey by Imak

BOOKS BY JULIAN DUTTON

Shakespeare's Journey Home: A Traveller's Guide Through Elizabethan England

Keeping Quiet: Visual Comedy in the Age of Sound

REVIEWS OF JULIAN DUTTON'S *KEEPING QUIET*

'... a lovingly compiled and thorough history of the genre beyond the advent of sound, writer and performer Julian Dutton extols the artistry of dumb-show, pantomime and slapstick... an absorbing, affectionate but critically rigorous account' – Jay Richardson, *Chortle*

'There's nothing funnier than visual comedy done well. And there's no more entertaining and informative book about its relevance today' – Bill Dare, creator *Dead Ringers*, BBC

'A custard pie in the face of those who say slapstick is dead, by the go-to writer of British visual comedy' – Harry Hill

Author's note: The word 'Gypsies' in the title is used generically as a term for nomadic or settled population groups choosing to live and work on rivers and canals, and not to describe any ethnic community.

There should be many contented spirits on board, for such
a life is both to travel and to stay at home … and for the
bargee, in his floating home, 'travelling abed,' it is merely
as if he were listening to another man's story or turning the
leaves of a picture book in which he had no concern.

– R.L. Stevenson, *An Inland Voyage*

A narrowboat family, 1874.

'Have you also learned that secret from the river;
that there is no such thing as time?'

Hermann Hesse, Siddhartha

September Sunshine, by George Dunlop Leslie.

CONTENTS

FOREWORD
BY SAMUEL WEST

I've never understood why motorways were introduced to Britain without a national debate. It was simply assumed that people wanted to live their lives faster, and get where they were going in the shortest possible time. I'm not so sure.

Imagine a time when rivers, not roads, were the DNA strands that gave Britain its personality. When canals, not railways, were the chosen way of cargo. A track that fords a stream gives a place a reason to exist. Over centuries, the reasons are made solid in wood, iron and brick; take to the stream and the reasons will show you their purpose. On day one you might feel itchy. Persevere, and the life of the waterways will slowly seep into you. Its slowness is its strength. Your heart beats to the speed of the water, the regular slog of the locks, the birds and insects that accompany you. You notice things more.

As our lives get faster and more digital, the desire to slow down and connect with the world outside grows. My parents, Timothy West and Prunella Scales, have very different attitudes to travel. He wants to round a new corner every day; she likes the comfort of familiar surroundings. It wasn't until halfway through their lives that they realised they could have both if they travelled by water. Seeing Britain by canal – from backstage, as it were – has been one of their greatest pleasures since. As my father points out: at three miles an hour, if anything goes wrong you can always walk where you were going quicker. They've now had a narrowboat for more than thirty years. The vagaries of age (and in my mother's case, dementia) only make them long for time on it more. It fits their shabby-bohemian need sometimes to be on the edges of society. Actors know that feeling well.

But however keen the family is on life on a canal boat, we always stopped short of making it permanent. The challenges of keeping a boat clean, tidy, safe (especially when children and now grand- and even great-grand-children join you on the voyage) are considerable. And it's HARD. I will sing the praises of a canal holiday to anyone, but I never pretend it's not a workout.

Most of the working families and liveaboards that Julian Dutton cele-brates in this wonderful book never had a 'real' home to return to. Their life was their work, and now that working boats have gone, it's good to know more about what's been lost. Then, as now, boat people were a tribe. A mix of Romany, ancient river traders, ex-miners and small farmers would migrate to where the work was, suffer when it wasn't, and live and die on what they called 'the Cut'. But beware the 'semi-rustic idyll', Dutton warns us: life for a canal family was often dark, cramped, unsanitary and dangerous.

The temptation of a life aboard has always been disproportionate. Even in the 1930s, when A. P. Herbert wrote his classic *The Water Gipsies*, it felt like a vanishing world. Luckily, campaigners kept many from closure and a life 'deep, rich and valuable' was saved.

Julian Dutton grew up on a houseboat and there could be no better or more informative guide to a history of life aboard. Whether you want to know about working boats, prison hulks, Dickensian houseboats, pleasure cruisers, floating restaurants or artists' retreats, this book is for you. He's particularly good on the story of bohemian Chelsea collectives that grew up after the Second World War, because of course it's his story too.

Nowadays water-living is as expensive as land, and mooring fees have homogenised communities just as rising rents do elsewhere. A shame. We need the outsiders of the Cut, living on the edge, throwing darts at the landlubbers. I think perhaps they know something we don't.

INTRODUCTION

Rivers have often invoked a dream state for poets and writers. For Kenneth Grahame in *Wind in the Willows* the Thames was a living thing that 'chattered on to him, a babbling procession of the best stories in the world, sent from the heart of the earth to be told at last to the insatiable sea'. The poet Shelley in 1817 wrote an entire epic work, *Laon and Cythna*, whilst drifting in a boat beneath the overhanging willows of Bisham near Great Marlow. Jerome K. Jerome's bestselling *Three Men in a Boat* (also written in Marlow) is perhaps the ultimate 'getting away from it all' novel, and it is to the river that he and his companions, weighed down with late nineteenth-century civilisation, flee in order to satiate their longing for escape.

Is it this dream state, this liberation from the trammels of ordinary consciousness, that people seek when they choose to leave the land behind and live on the water? Or perhaps it is a quest to answer a deep ancestral call, to reawaken buried instincts: somewhere far inside the soul of an accountant a voice pleads 'you must abandon these dry figures, and go off to sail, drift and fish' – and the price of not heeding that voice is to suffer at best a restless discontent, at worst a spiritual death.

Whatever has impelled people to leave behind 'ordinary life' and take to the water, the history of the houseboat is an evolution from necessity to choice, and tracing its line all the way from the fisherfolk of ancient times to the bohemian artists and writers of post-war England and beyond, to the current wave of some 30,000 liveaboards, is to delineate a unique and fascinating seam of British history. In almost every history book, living and working afloat achieves at most only a passing mention, despite being an important part of British life for centuries. There are numerous works on the history of canals and rivers, yet most focus exclusively on the economic and industrial dimension; none tell the complete social history of the life and lore of those hundreds of thousands of Britons who over the past two millennia and beyond have spent their lives adrift.

This book attempts to fill that gap. Its aim is to chronicle a way of life dating back to prehistory. From the trading vessel where a sailor or merchant might live for weeks aboard his craft, to the generations of canal bargees plying their narrowboats along the industrial arteries of the nation for centuries until the railway – and later road haulage – signalled their decline, to the post-war baby boomers of the 1950s seeking a different lifestyle to that of orthodox mainstream society, and contemporary families searching for a more economic form of homeowning when house prices are challenging a whole new generation, the story of houseboat dwelling on the waterways of Britain is a rich and varied one, containing as many twists and turns as the riverways they have chosen to make their home.

The necessity began, of course, in the pre-Iron Age settlements before the invention of agriculture, when hunting and gathering meant a coast-hugging life of fishing or, for the inland tribes, harvesting the rivers and lakes. And what easier way to gather aquatic sustenance than by living on the water itself? Ghostly remnants of these water-borne villages still dot the British Isles – the blunted remains of jetties supporting long-vanished huts, the occasional glimpse of oak foundations when tides recede. At Llangorse Lake in Brecon one can experience a fine reconstruction of one of these 'floating villages', stretching out across the glistening waters richly inhabited by plump fish of all kinds, to be gathered daily by families living right above their quarry: stout piers supporting habitations whose foundations were buried deep in the mud of the lake or riverbed. Not strictly 'houseboats' on the lakes so falling outside the scope of this book, but the coastal folk trawling the oceans of this island would often travel for days, seeking the extensive shoals further offshore, living aboard. It is these anglers, along with inland traders stretching from the Neolithic age onwards, who are the ancestors of our modern houseboat dweller.

While the river traders who traversed the Thames, Severn and Trent in ancient and medieval times were the first historic 'houseboat' dwellers, the first modern liveaboards were the inhabitants of the man-made waterways when canal mania carved the country with hundreds of man-made 'cuts' criss-crossing the nation. These arteries carried tonnages to the growing industrial centres of the nation, and in so doing created two things: Britain as the first powerhouse of the world and the boat as a place of permanent dwelling. In the period between 1760 and 1840 when railways displaced canals as the prime mode of industrial transport, people flowed from the land to the water, and thousands of families began a life afloat, lasting many generations right up to the 1960s (as late as 1964 life on the canal was still considered a sufficiently widely known way of life for Associated British Pictures to release *The Bargee*, a comedy about a canal worker starring Harry H. Corbett – admittedly a film that served as a eulogy to the way of life, but nevertheless a marvellous portrait of the dying days of canal living).

The first major modern boat dwellers, then, were the canal folk, whose homes traversed the country between the growing coal centres of Britain, fuelling the nation with steam power and eventually lighting all cities and towns with coal gas. As early as 1768 the promotion of the boat over the horse was noted in the House of Commons, its Journal proclaiming that, 'one horse will draw as much upon a navigable canal as one hundred will draw upon a turnpike road.' Such an elevation of the boat as supreme carrier of the nation bestowed an importance on the boat dweller that lasted nearly a century, for even when rail had overtaken the canals, water-borne trade continued as a driving force of British trade, albeit a weakened one as rail and road became supreme.

If the story of the canal boat as place of residence for the bargee and their family is a fascinating one, the development of the houseboat as an act of choice in pursuit of an 'alternative lifestyle' in the twentieth century is equally rich, and of huge cultural import. In the period up to the 1940s there was still extensive river-borne trade along the Thames, but along-side these working families plying their wares along the waterways the new century saw the rise of the non-commercial houseboat, many famous devotees of aquatic living giving credence and not a little notoriety to this alternative way of life. Noted barrister and author A.P. Herbert was one such legendary figure, famously residing with his family on a barge moored at Hammersmith. Whilst being known as a humourist, Herbert's books on houseboat life were equally well received, his novel *The Water Gipsies* (1930) figuring high in the canon of houseboat fiction. It is Herbert's life too that advertised the important role of the houseboat in war, for during the 1939–45 conflict houseboats, including his own, were enlisted in the hugely important River Emergency Service, undergoing patrols and other vital war work up and down the Thames and other British rivers.

In the post-war years the houseboat became bohemian and slightly raffish, a place of beat poetry, bottle parties and film actors: Dorothy Tutin famously inhabited a London barge, and films such as *The Horse's Mouth* with Alec Guinness and *The Naked Truth* with Peter Sellers and Terry-Thomas made the floating villages of London famous on the big screen. I myself caught the ebbing tide of this wave of houseboat living, being born on a boat moored in Cheyne Walk, Chelsea, and growing up in the 1960s in what is now known as Chelsea Reach – and was, indeed, inspired to write this book when I made a return visit, years later, to this floating village.

I wondered how the years had wrought their changes on this little pocket of 1950s bohemia, this ensemble of actors, artists and boozers, this much-sought-after locale of films such as *The Spy Who Came in from the Cold* and many more. Who now was living in the boat where I used to sit on deck as a boy and watch the clouds of smoke from nearby Lots Road Power Station, or wave to the barges chugging past the Chelsea Flour Mills? Who now was being rocked to sleep by the ebb and flow of the Thames, the smell of boat tar, cracked leather and paraffin in the nostrils, feeling all the time that we were on a camping trip yet only yards from the King's Road? Had houseboat living changed in the intervening half-century?

My return journey to the houseboat community where I grew up led me to make further investigations into the history of living afloat, and out of those investigations this book was born.

Chelsea Reach differs from many other houseboat communities in that none of the craft are narrowboats – they are mostly wide-beamed converted landing craft bought up by an enterprising marine owner in 1945. None has the cramped feel of the canal barge and most have two floors. Despite the size of the dwellings, however, the air of a shanty town still lingers. Growing up here in the 1960s I have dim but possibly apocryphal memories of wives beating washing on the stones revealed by the morning tide, much like folk on the banks of the Ganges. We lived on top of each other, borrowed each other's food, money and clothes, heard each other's parties, rows and intimacies. But who lived there now?

It took me ten minutes to navigate the busy traffic of Cheyne Walk, but as with all houseboat communities, as soon as you approach you enter a different, quieter world: hidden behind the huge Thames wall, reached only by gangplanks, here was Chelsea Reach – a world apart, a village in magical isolation, almost like Brigadoon.

The river is wide here between Battersea Bridge and Sands End, mud-brown and peculiarly desolate, contrasting violently with the warm, colourful nest of houseboats tethered to its bank. One is hit by the sudden, warm stench of a mossy grey river smell, a scent familiar to me from childhood. Also unchanged are the serpents of twisted steel ropes snaking through the sloppy mud, lashing their hulking charges to the great rusting iron rings sunk into the slimy Thames wall. The colours of the boats too had not altered – fairground pinks, flame, violet with gold curlicues, rich purples, curved splashes of flamboyant rose – an echo of the exotic boat-painting tradition from centuries gone by. And the names – *The Patriarch*, *The Odyssey*, *The Dinty Moore*, *The Kandy-Koloured Tangerine* …

And the *Moby Dick*, my birthplace? Living there now is a graphic artist couple; their neighbour is a barrister, and next door but one is 'a lovely couple: he's a production executive and she's a production designer', and they have 'full plumbing and electricity'. The only remnant of the old days is a tank-duct for the chemical toilets. The Flour Mills further down the bank are gone, replaced of course with luxury flats. And the rent? Several thousand a month. (My parents bought our boat in 1958 for £500.) A vessel here will set you back a minimum of half a million.

And yet, for all these changes, one vital thing has not altered, and that is the social diversity of the occupants; indeed, the one thing they have in common is the impulse and desire to live afloat. It is an impulse borne from the need to live a different kind of life, away from mainstream society. Boat living attracts people from all sorts of backgrounds, rich, poor, the ambitious and the wastrel, the artist and the inventor. It is the desire to occupy a place outside the stream of normal belonging, where one wakes not to the sound of car horns or refuse lorries but to the whisper of the river, the song of the wind through the trees on the banks, the chatter of waterfowl. It is a perennial impulse that drives people to keep one foot firmly in nature, in a little bit of wilderness, as an antidote to the sometimes stifling effects of a suffocating modernity. E.G.R. Taylor, reviewing W.G. Hoskins' seminal work *The Making of the English Landscape*, wrote that he:

> views the industrial revolution with mounting horror, and the industrialists themselves are bitterly chastised as completely and grotesquely insensitive. Hoskins has happily moved to a quiet spot in Oxfordshire where he ... looks out of his study window on to the past, (and) draws for us a last tender and evocative picture of the gentle unravished English landscape, and forgetting all the horrors, reaches back through the centuries one by one and rediscovers Eden.

It is that call, that inward impulse, that yearning for Eden, that thousands of British people have listened to across the centuries, and obeyed. It is that impulse that is the beating heart of this chronicle, the story of the British houseboat and life on Britain's rivers and canals.

I

INTO THE
WILDERNESS

In the late 1880s the writer and sailor Joseph Conrad was gazing out from the deck of the yawl *Nellie* moored near Gravesend. With a stub of pencil he jotted down some notes for a novel he was planning, *Heart of Darkness*. He wrote:

> The sea-reach of the Thames stretched before us like the beginning of an interminable waterway. In the offing the sea and the sky were welded together without a joint, and in the luminous space the tanned sails of the barges drifting up with the tide seemed to stand still in red clusters of canvas sharply peaked, with gleams of varnished sprits.

Conrad knew he was looking centuries back in time. For the sails of England's riverboats were truly tanned, and had been since time immemorial, caked with the distinctive ochre pigment of horse fat, cod oil and seawater, turning the inland waterways of Britain into a flowing forest of reddish brown.

Conrad goes on to imagine what a Roman might have seen on his first encounter with ancient Britain: swamp, mist, lowlands carpeted with forest – essentially a wilderness. London did not exist, being an estuary of swampland and thick woodland stretching to the north and west on deep beds of clay.

No bridge crossed the Thames. The Romans laid down the foundations of Londinium only by dint of the two gravel spurs making that part of the river fordable. If those two spurs had been situated 30 miles upstream, the capital would have been Maidenhead. The very existence of any inland settlements, let alone towns or villages, lay far in the distant future, and would owe their birth and growth solely to the waterways that ran through their locality. Apart from the occasional man-made mound, barrow, cairn and isolated farming communities of stone huts and thatch, Britain's landscape was wild. Even as late as the Elizabethan era travellers would describe the country between towns as 'heath and wilderness'. From the very beginnings it was the inland waterways of this country that dictated the entire geography of human settlement and activity in the ensuing centuries.

It is in this wilderness that the houseboat is born.

The Dover Boat, sailed by Bronze Age traders. At 3,500 years old, it is Britain's earliest vessel. (Dover Museum)

The Romans had long known that Britain was a boating nation. The first-century writer Lucan writes in his *Pharsalia* (also known as *The Civil War*):

When Sicoris kept his banks, the shallop light
Of hoary willow bark they build, which bent
On hides of oxen, bore the weight of man
And swam the torrent. Thus on sluggish Po
Venetians float; and on th' encircling sea
Are borne Britannia's nations.

It's an extraordinary eulogy to the ancient coracle, or *curragh*, bearing testament to the robustness of Britain's international reputation for seamanship, for while Venetians drift idly down the 'sluggish' Po, Britons brave the oceans. Other historians bear witness to British sailors traversing the North Atlantic in the humble leather-bound vessels.

Brave though the Ancient Britons may have been, when we travel back in time to those ancient days beyond the Roman conquest it is important not to downplay the dangers of travel by water, and to adopt vicariously the very real fears and anxieties many of our ancestors would have harboured towards the rivers of this island. Compared to prehistoric times our rivers are now (relatively) tamed, domesticated, parcelled, with locks and weirs controlling the flow, man-made embankments cauterising floods (in many cases), and fragrant towpaths occupying the margins of the waterways where once woods and forests hid wolves, bears and other predators. For our ancestors, to set out on the river was often to take one's life in one's hands, submit to the fitful whimsy of wild current, waterfall, or attack both animal and human. There were many reasons that inspired or compelled our ancestors to overcome these perils and travel and live on the waterways – migration from hostile tribes, fishing for subsistence and trade.

It is only the latter – trade – that began the slow creation of what was to become a significant subculture of 'live-afloats', and it is that subculture that we are setting out to trace from prehistoric times to the present day.

The first true 'houseboat dwellers', then, were traders, and the earliest characters in the long story of living afloat are those who took to the water in a primitive vessel – large dugouts, and then wider vessels made from several dugouts attached by horizontal planks – probably loaded with Neolithic axe heads from one of the many 'factories' to another part of the country. The journey of these early liveaboards, though inland, was nevertheless not without peril.

It is only through this lens of danger that we can gain a true picture of what our forefathers felt towards the waterways that have snaked through Britain since the retreat of the ice 10,000 years ago. To our ancestors, nature was untamed, full of gods and unseen forces to be feared and placated. It is a short mental step from fear to placation and devotion. To find out precisely how ancient Britons felt one can do worse than observe contemporary Hindus of India, who to this day descend the stone steps (ghats) of their towns along the banks of the Ganges every morning to bathe and give worship.

Such votive reverence would have been the same for our ancestors. Even in the post-pagan Middle Ages pilgrim effigies – small crudely carved statuettes – were tossed into the Thames; in pre-Christian times to supplicate gods, in Christian times Saints, the reverence is the same.

The worship of water is as old as history. And this imputing of divine or supernatural qualities to waterways lingers to this day. Even as late as 1882 during a search for a drowned woman in the River Derwent at Milford, people took with them a drum which they beat over the water. Tradition held that at the point where the drum gave forth no sound, there lay the body. To this day, supernatural powers are projected onto natural phenomena, such as the *Aegir* of the River Trent, a high spring tide meeting the downstream flow that causes a high bore wave that for centuries has swept unsuspecting folk to their deaths. The ghosts, gods and monsters of the rivers are sometimes nurturing, sometimes avenging, to be appeased or thanked accordingly.

As with the waterways, so too the craft. Even now vessels are launched onto the rivers and seas with a mysterious ceremony, including the breaking of the 'neck' of a bottle, thought to be an echo of the human sacrifice sometimes made before a water-borne journey. The entire lore of boats is steeped in folklore, superstition and ritual, and will be etched throughout this book.

That the earliest human settlements grew up along rivers and streams is a nexus founded upon the blindingly basic need for fresh water and fish, so it is but a small step from the prehistoric village to the use of boats. Fiona M.

Haughey in *People and Water: A Study of the Relationship Between Humans and Rivers in the Mesolithic and Neolithic with Particular Reference to that within the Thames Basin* (University College London, 2009) references the visible link between the construction of cairns and the direction of travel of rivers and other waterways, indicating that whatever future purposes cairns evolved – such as burials – their prime purpose was as landmarks, demarcators of routes. In short, in a landscape largely forested and inhabited by predators the cairn showed the 'way out', a beacon signalling a relatively safe route from the hunting grounds to the uplands, as well as being a 'guide back' to travellers and traders, tangentially, or even fundamentally, flagging up the proximity of water supply.

In any history of boat dwelling, mention must be made of the Iron Age 'Lake Villages' of Britain, of which Glastonbury and Llangorse near the Brecon Beacons are shining examples. Though not strictly living in the vessels, the inhabitants of these water-borne communities would reach their abodes purely by water. Glastonbury, the best preserved prehistoric village in Europe, was discovered by Arthur Bulleid in 1892; it was not strictly a lake but was created at the edge of a patch of birch, alder and willow trees, in the midst of a large swamp of reed, sedge, open water and wet woodland. Through numerous channels in this swamp the sluggish waters of the River Brue slowly headed north, towards the Axe valley. As well as the abundance of fish and birds for sustenance, the water dwelling in this instance was primarily for defence. But trade was perhaps also a factor: the site may have been located on an important water-borne trade route from central Somerset to the Severn Estuary. A dugout canoe was found in the foundations and another one in a nearby field.

Another, though perhaps later, 'artificial island' can be found on Llangorse Lake in the Brecons in Wales. A *crannog*, about 130ft from the north shore, was constructed of massive planks of oak behind which was built a dwelling platform formed from layers of stone, soil and brushwood. Again, the only access is clearly by boat. The occupants would, as at Glastonbury, have survived on the unusual abundance of the teeming fish and bird life in and around the waters. It is more difficult to date Llangorse, though the existence of an Iron Age fort on the hillside overlooking the lake would indicate an ancient settlement.

The Lake Village, Glastonbury, home of Britain's earliest inland water dwellers.

From the first, then, our ancestors lived and worked by water, a knowledge of navigation evolving as an elemental skill hardwired into their DNA. Christopher Tilley, in his *A Phenomenology of Landscape, 1994*, observed that:

> River systems, their place within the landscape (which changes as the water flows through the various localities), their rate of flow, their shallowness or deepness, and their life-giving properties, are all things which will have influenced human activity within the landscape both in a materialistic or practical capacity but also in an experiential or symbolic way.

In short, our use of waterways for utilitarian purposes of survival was inextricably linked to a supra-rational – what might be called spiritual – reverence.

It is but a short step from this primordial relationship with water to the historical fact that the boat is a far, far more ancient invention than the wheeled cart.

The old demarcations of our prehistory still hold – stone, bronze, iron – and it is, of course, to traders in these metals that we must first herald as this country's earliest 'houseboat' dwellers. While trade boomed in the ages of bronze and iron, Neolithic trade was not by any means niggardly, and evidence that river traders were using boats as accommodation exists as far back as 3000 BC. Large 'axe factories' dotted the country, producing flint axe heads either in finished or as 'rough-outs' – a half-finished state – indicating that even from earliest times division of labour was already a widely adopted technique of production. Evidence for a widespread system of internal trade can be inferred from the fact that a greenstone axe head from Cornwall was among the offerings found at Grime's Graves, far away in eastern England. There, some 4,000 tons of flint were mined between 2600 and 1500 BC, from pits sunk up to 42ft deep through chalk to reach the high-quality black flint 'floor stone'. Usable flint was more readily available on the surface, but tools made from mined flint appear to have had a special significance.

At Grime's Graves and Langdale, stone tools left the site as rough-outs that would be polished elsewhere. How, where and what the finished products were traded for is uncertain. But axe heads are frequently found at Neolithic causewayed enclosure meeting places like Windmill Hill, which were the sites of large-scale feasting for the living and ceremonies for the dead. They have also been found at Castlerigg Stone Circle in Cumbria, which might have been a significant stop on a trading route.

Prehistory, of course, is a span of time vaster than our historical, literate age: when we envision the journey between the Palaeolithic and the Iron Age we are discussing 10,000 years. It is important then not to assume one single landscape throughout this era but a constantly evolving one, shaped by mines, long-distance trade routes, green lanes, cairns, stone circles and numerous artificial mounds.

The key historical engine of the expansion of river trade was, of course, the transition of Britain's population from hunter-gatherer to farmer, which took place in these islands approximately 4,000 years ago: gradually the nomadic follower of animal herds became a rare figure in the landscape, replaced by settled tribes of farmers, manufacturers and traders. As agriculture became the prime economic activity of our ancestors the use of these flint tools metamorphosed from hunting and treatment of animal skins to wood-clearing and building. The transportation of these tons of flint tools combined land routes with waterways. Geologists in 2015 not only confirmed that the inner bluestones of Stonehenge had their origin as the Preseli hills of Pembrokeshire but have also identified the actual quarry, Craig Rhos-y-felin. The fact that the quarry lies on the north side of Preseli has thrown into doubt the previous theory that the stones were transported by river or sea – conjecture is now pointing to what is now the A40 – but this does not rule out inland aquatic trade as a major activity of our enterprising forefathers. The Phoenicians are well known to have established a trading empire stretching from Greece to the Canary Islands to southern Britain, particularly Cornwall.

As this Middle Eastern empire waned, other merchants sought out Britain's shores and established important trade routes for local populations of river folk. Imported exotic goods – including amber from the Baltic and gold from Ireland – have been discovered in Bronze Age round barrows, suggesting that there were established European trading networks. By the later Iron Age, southern England's principal trading partners were northern Gaul (France) and Armorica (Brittany). Hengistbury Head in Dorset became a thriving port, probably exchanging locally smelted iron for goods such as figs, glass, tools, pottery and above all jars of wine, imported either via Brittany or directly from Italy.

What were the people like? When Julius Caesar invaded in 54 bc he described British tribes as being similar in many ways to those he had encountered in Gaul and elsewhere, though he did note that when venturing beyond the relative wealth of southern Britain there were many who 'still fed on flesh and milk', in other words, tribes who had not settled easily into a life of crop-growing and harvesting.

And their boats? Well, it is here, when discussing prehistory, that archaeology almost fails us. Boats, by nature of their construction from wood, have come down to us in niggardly scraps. Setting the ubiquitous hide and woven-wood coracle aside, roughly sketched, the story of the riverboat is an evolution from trunk to plank, from dugout to clinker-built, for before tools were invented to hew wood into flat boards, every vessel was either gouged tree or lashed logs – raft or canoe. The world's oldest extant boat is the Pesse canoe: 9,000 years old and pockmarked with flint or antler marks, it lay preserved in a peat bog in the Netherlands until exposed during the construction of the A28 motorway. There is no reason to doubt that this crude, basic design was a similar template for British river-goers, which along with the animal-skin coracle was the aquatic Model T Ford of the waterways for millennia until the plank was born and larger, more ambitious vessels were constructed.

Every single Roman boat discovered by archaeologists in Britain is a trading vessel. (For the purposes of this book all boats that were engaged in long-distance trade will be regarded as *houseboats*, for the very reason that those sailing would live aboard, and given the difficulties of navigating the inland waterways in ancient and medieval times, journeys took several weeks.)

Bronze Age vessels were clinker-built with sewn planks – oak timber lashed together with strands of yew. If the dugout canoe was the ancestor of the punt then the sewn-plank longboat of the Bronze Age is the forerunner of the inland barge. Twenty examples of these more sophisticated boats have been found in Britain – notably three at Ferriby in the East Riding of Yorkshire and one in Norwest Holst near Dover. The River Dour is a chalk stream that flows from Temple Ewell in Kent to what was once a large estuary near Dover – now culverted. The Dover Boat at 3,500 years old is considered to be the oldest surviving seafaring boat in the world and was clearly built for the channel, probably for trade with what became Gaul. Riverboats, of course, had to be of shallower draught, to navigate the often low and changeable reaches of the waterways, not to mention the treacherous waterfalls.

Many history books covering the early centuries of the first millennia include the dramatic phrase 'the coming of the Romans', and this present volume is no exception. The aim of this book is not to linger on a litany and recitation of dry generalities but to focus on the living, breathing realities of boat life in Britain. In order to comprehend the growth of what we now call the 'houseboat', however, one has first to etch in broad strokes the historical background to the extraordinary expansion of Italic civilisation.

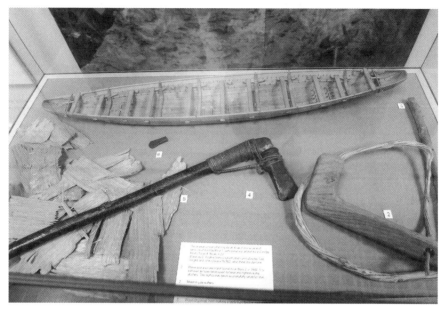

At 4,000 years old, the Ferriby Boats, coastal and inland traders, are Europe's most ancient houseboats. (Hull Museum)

To the Romans, Britain was of course a far-flung outcrop of the empire, the last territory to be conquered. For Julius Caesar the curious island on the north-west of his dominions was always a challenge. It was a natural sea-protected fortress. The relatively civilised Belgic tribes in the southern parts were not a huge threat but the northern fiefdoms had gained a reputation for ferocity and strength, particularly the Cornovii tribe in what are now Cheshire and Shropshire, whose military prowess led them post-conquest to become the only Celtic tribe to form a legion of the Roman army, the *Cohors Primae Cornoviorus.*

Yet conquer Britain they did, and within a few decades elephants were a common sight in Colchester. Despite a few outbursts of resistance from stubborn British kings and queens such as Caratacus and Boadicea, the isle of Albion had fallen.

What effect did the Romans have on the growth of what we now call the houseboat? Once again the key word is trade. The principal engine of expansion in water-borne trade in the centuries from AD 43 to 480, when the empire collapsed, was the huge influx of not only the military but also a class of settling Romans with a taste for luxury goods and materials. It is estimated that the occupying armies alone required 100,000 acres merely to supply them with cereal crops, one legion alone consuming 500 bushels a week. And not only cereal: the Roman diet was a broad range of meat, fish, fruit and vegetables. This led to two things that created a veritable renaissance of the boat-dweller: first, a massive increase in agricultural production; and secondly, all these comestibles had to be transported – some were imported but most needed to be carried from other parts of Britain, by simple dint of them being consumables with a limited life. How did Iron Age Britain cope with this rapid increase in population and demand? Historians are divided on how indigenous farmers stepped up, but the fact that three quarters of the population were in agriculture is a supportive factor. Also, the presence of extensive Celtic grain-storage pits indicates that production for surplus was, in all probability, incentivised by the Roman influx.

The growth of road transport in the centuries following the Roman invasion and settlement is one of the best-known and widely lauded logistical achievements of the empire; this has led to a consequent – and mistaken – relegation of water transport to a secondary consideration. This is far from a complete picture. The cold fact was that transporting goods by water in the ancient world was 15 per cent cheaper than taking it by road, this in spite of the huge advances made in the quality of highways. There is an argument to be made that the very magnitude of their approach to road-building betrays a hint of desperation, implying a need not quite being met. It is clear from the fact that all the Roman boats found in Britain by archaeologists are merchant vessels that there was a sophisticated inland-waterways system, meaning that life afloat for Britons had entered a new phase. M.I. Finley delivers an authoritative argument for the supremacy of water transport over roads in *The Ancient Economy*, 1973:

> The ox was the chief traction animal of antiquity, the mule and donkey his near rivals, the horse hardly at all. All three are slow and hungry. The transport figures in Diocletian's edict of maximum prices imply that a 1200-pound wagon-load of wheat would double in price in 300 miles, that a shipment of grain by sea from one end of the Mediterranean to the other would cost less (ignoring the risks) than

carting it seventy-five miles. A state could afford to engage ox-teams for the extraordinary purpose of shifting marble column-drums for temples, employing on an average thirty yoke for each drum ... But individuals could not move bulky merchandise long distances by land as a normal activity, nor could any but the wealthiest and most powerful communities. Most necessities are bulky – cereals, pottery, metals and timber – and so towns could not safely outgrow the food production of their own hinterlands unless they had direct access to waterways. Not even the famed Roman roads, built for military and political, not commercial reasons, made any significant difference, since the means of traction remained the same. It was the many rivers of Gaul (and Britain) that elicited comment from Roman writers and facilitated the growth of inland cities.

When in doubt, follow the money: if transporting goods by water was 15 per cent of the cost of conveying it overland, then by water it went. To elevate Finley's belief from mere conjecture to fact one has only to look at the prevalence of oyster shells in every far-flung corner of Britain, from Wessex to the Wash, from Silchester to Hadrian's Wall. Because of the shelf life of these delectable molluscs, it is impossible to convey them by road – they would have to have been preserved in water.

So towns and cities began springing up on the banks of navigable rivers up and down the country, many owing their very existence to water trade and stimulating the consequent growth of a permanent river-dwelling population. Whether it was transporting grain and timber to London or pewter from the south-west, Britain became locked into the network of a vast trading empire. Huge wharves were built on the Thames in London, with great quays stretching for a kilometre. The remains of river craft and coastal ships have been dredged from riverbeds, one notable craft being salvaged from Blackfriars in 1962 still containing a Domitian coin deliberately placed into the socket where the mast was placed, dating the vessel to AD 88–89.

A key component of Roman trade was of course not strictly trade at all, but rather *tax*. Grain tax – the ancestor of the medieval tithe – existed throughout the empire, and Britain was no exception. And the waterways dictated the type of boats that developed. To use the small canals and canalised rivers a particular

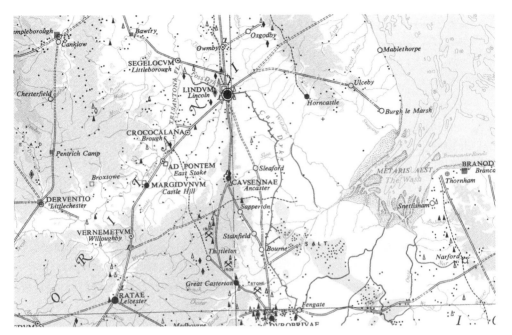

Roman Britain, showing the Fosse Dyke, connecting the River Trent at Torksey to Lincoln and Car Dyke – possibly Britain's oldest man-made waterways.

kind of vessel would be needed, for example not more than 4–5ft wide or 15ft long in order to negotiate the small streams leading to the Kennet.

Alongside the natural cargoes – grain, wine, meat – Roman Britain was a manufacturing province. Every day thousands of rivermen and women would load up their vessels with cattle hides, timber for joists, floors, roofs, door frames and furniture, and of course fuel. The construction of hundreds of watermills was a contributory factor to what historians suspect to be a major deforestation, which is perhaps why, by the second and third centuries, coal began to supplement wood, as indicated by the increase in the number of open-cast mines. Coal was a huge internal good, and vast supplies were carried by boat to the Roman fortresses at Chester at Heronbridge, and throughout the country for heating systems. Other major cargoes were metals of all kinds – gold, silver, iron, lead, copper, tin – and building stone, far more easily carried by water than by road. We have referred to the immense cost of transporting goods by land, and much evidence points to scarcely any stone being imported during the Roman period apart from specialist materials for mosaics, the bulk of it being mined locally in huge quarries.

But perhaps the most ubiquitous goods to be transported by Britain's first river dwellers, given its survival and consequent visibility in many domestic and military archaeological sites, was pottery. Huge army contracts fuelled a surge in demand, and whilst finer ware such as Samian or 'terra sigillata' were imported from Gaul and beyond, the bulk of the more basic coarse ceramics were manufactured domestically. Just as centuries later when the coming of the canals facilitated the growth of the Potteries in Staffordshire – what easier way to transport fragile goods but by water? – productive pottery sites in the Roman era grew up alongside waterways. And once the skills of British potters caught up with their continental counterparts, and in many cases overtook them, it wasn't long before local industry was producing both the coarse and fine wares that met the demand of a growing population. Peterborough, with its excellent access to the Fenland water-ways as well as the River Nene, became a productive hub of this river-borne trade. Soon boatmen were carrying barge-loads of clay-ware daily to every corner of the province and beyond. Excavations of the nearby Roman town of Chesterton, also lying near the Nene, reveal an extensive industrial site, and this region was by the fourth century joined by Headington in Oxford, whose kilns – unearthed from beneath the site of the Churchill Hospital – fired the thousands of fine and coarse ware transported by Thames boatmen to London and beyond by the second century.

Pottery and other fragile goods were transported by road as well as water, of course, but historians note the significant fact that some of the largest production sites, the Nene Valley and Oxford, were near riverways. In the case of Oxford, Peter Salway in *Roman Britain* (Oxford, Clarendon Press 1981) states:

> [there is] a contention that certain sites far from the centre of pro-duction seem to have a far greater proportion of Oxford wares than their general distribution would make one expect. Since these sites are near good water communications with Oxford, then the cheapness of water transport is the likely cause. If this is true, then perhaps the

reason why the Oxford industry grew so large in the first place and was thus able to compete exceptionally well was because cheap transport allowed it to build up an initial market on a large scale. This would have provided working capital for further expansion.

It is not fanciful hyperbole to assert, then, that a large group of itinerant boat people had been expanded – if not created – by the stimulus of Roman conquest, infrastructure, town growth and population.

Yet rivers were only part of this growth – the Romans also built canals. The question of the extent of Roman construction of man-made waterways in Britain tests historians to this day. For example, the Caer Dyke that runs for 85 miles along the western edge of the Fens was described by William Stukeley in the eighteenth century as being a goods-transporting waterway, and indeed remains of a Roman boat have been found at Waterbeach along with a cargo of pottery from Horningsea. But other historians point to unnavigable stretches of the Caer that do not reach the levels of sophistication of the canal it is connected to, the Foss Dyke, which is clearly a purpose-built conveyor of goods. The Foss Dyke connects the rivers Witham and Trent, near Torksey, for just over 11 miles to Lincoln, and incredibly was still in use more than 1,500 years later when it was in the ownership of the London & North Eastern Railway.

The economic and industrial expansion in Roman Britain, then, is the backdrop to the rise of the river trader, and once established these itinerant, almost vagabond dwellers on the water, became a permanent part of the British landscape.

But what was daily life like for one of these ancient water folk? Let us observe a boat travelling between Oxford and London with a cargo of pottery.

First, what was their boat like? As aforementioned, a trading vessel was a houseboat in all but name, for the crew would spend a week or more aboard. What settlements and villages did they pass on their journey? What did they eat? What did they get paid? What did they see in London when they disembarked their loads? And what did they bring back?

While the perennial Ancient British coracle, or *curragh*, of tanned leather on a basket of woven willow sealed with waterproofing tree-sap tar, lasted for centuries – indeed, in some part of Wales coracle-fishing endured until the late twentieth century – it is clear that the bulky goods of the Roman Empire required more robust and larger vessels with shallow draughts capable of navigating Britain's untamed and often dangerous rivers.

The solution was the appearance of what can be described as an 'expanded log boat', the ancestor of the flat-bottomed barge, consisting of a widened version of the single hollowed log with horizontal girders fixing the expansion and supplying rigidity, and overlapping, or clinker-built planks providing strength. Examples of these are the Ferriby boats found on the Humber by Ted Wright between 1937 and 1962. These have been dated as early as 2000 BC, so pre-Roman, but the classic 'Celtic' design of nailed planks was superseded by the stitched vessel by the time the Romans landed, and clinker-built soon became the template for river traders' craft.

A barge, then, of approximately 40ft in length, manned by several men and possibly women. In later medieval times, right up to the age of canals, it was traditional to have boys aboard as apprentices, so that might also have been the case in Roman Britain. Carts would bring the pottery from Headington to the swampy margins of the Thames, and the boat crew would load up the wares in straw-lined caskets, lashed to the centre of the boat with leather fastenings. A crude cabin in the aft, with possible cooking facilities and primitive sleeping arrangements, though lesser crew would probably sleep on deck, protected by hides.

Oars push the boat out onto the shimmering water. No towpaths yet, for horsepower was a thing of the future. More importantly, there were no towns on the banks. The English town is essentially a medieval invention; in Roman times the principal physical unit of economy was the villa, more often than not situated in the countryside, near a fresh-water supply but rarely on the banks of rivers. From its position the proprietors of the villa, whether military or civilian, would glean goods, crops and wares from the surrounding land and scattered settlements. So for our Romano-British houseboat dweller market towns were a thing of the distant future. Flash locks, fishing weirs and watermills were among the few signs of civilisation our boat crew would have encountered on their way from Oxford to London, along with a few isolated farms and homesteads. Apart from these glimpses of humankind, the gliding Thames foreshore was mostly empty, wild and untamed.

Flash locks were a physical challenge for our crew. The more primitive forerunner of today's common pound lock, the flash lock was a crude method of stemming water flow and increasing depth by a series of vertical planks or 'rymers' that slotted into a horizontal beam of oak on the riverbed at a point in the waterway where the level rose or fell. Any downstream boat would wait for these rymers to be removed then shoot down in the sudden flash of water. Vessels travelling upstream would have to be winched up the elevation with a capstan wheel on the bank. Flash locks began to be replaced by pound locks (the division of the waterway with two gates allowing the boat to sit in the valley between, until the water level is raised allowing onward travel) from the sixteenth century onwards, and were a thing of the past by the nineteenth century.

With a precious cargo these flash locks were a risk, and our boat dwellers would have to exercise muscular and skilful navigation. Here, lifelong skills would be brought into play: knowledge of the changes in current, the rise and fall of the riverbed, waterfalls, outcrops of stone beneath dangerous weirs. This is perhaps why in later times the ferrymen of London,

The flash lock, forerunner to the pound lock: a challenge to every boatman and his family, with barges hauled up steep river inclines. (Ted Coles)

The last remaining flash-lock capstan wheel in Britain, on the Thames at Hurley.

who would carry passengers up the tidal Thames from the City as far as Twickenham and Hampton, were often of great age: old ferrymen were much in demand for their accumulated wisdom of the river.

In the days before river authorities and the Thames Conservancy, there were many competing elements on the rivers: local populations harvesting the fish with fishing weirs – barriers erected across-stream to herd shoals into the woven traps – were the enemies of passing boats, as were the hated keepers of the locks, who would often charge a despised tariff, as were the watermills, who though often situated on a tangential branch or mill stream off the main current, would disturb the river traders by the alteration of the flow. So loathed were the fish weirs that they earned a special mention in the Magna Carta, forming one of the Barons' key demands: 'All fish-weirs shall be removed from the Thames, the Medway, and throughout the whole of England, except on the sea coast' – proof that the status of the river trader, by 1215, had eclipsed that of the local populace.

With its twists and turns the Thames turned the journey from Oxford to London into a week-long voyage. No pleasant Thames-side inns – the boatmen would eat aboard or on the bank: wheat pancakes in the morning, fish and cold salted meat at midday, in the evening, porridge enriched with vegetables, fruit and meat. As they sailed so they must have fished, adding a fresh catch to their diet.

After a week or more travelling thus, our Romano-British crew would arrive at Fortress London – by AD 200 an impressive citadel with a population of 60,000. As has been noted, huge wharves and embankments of a kilometre in length stretched along the foreshore, leading trading boats into primitive docks and vast storehouses constructed on dry ground (right up to the latter part of the twentieth century the area between the wharf and the warehouse was known as 'Romeland'). On the home stretch prior to their arrival, our crew would have passed deep woodlands covering the clay slopes of what is now West London, reaching up to what became Notting Hill ('Nutting-Hill' – a forest of nut-trees), Thorney Island which was to become Westminster, prone to flooding until the Abbey and the embankment was built, the governor's palace fronting the water with its vast decking, the Temple of Mithras behind, the Cheapside Baths, the mighty forum just visible from the river on the upper slopes towards Bishopsgate – the largest forum in the Roman Empire north of the Alps – and surrounding it all, the vast city wall, enveloping the city that had by the second century supplanted Colchester as the greatest in Britain.

Our boat ties up at the vast wharf next to the old Roman wooden bridge that crossed to Southwark, or *south walk*, containing a scattering of settlements and trading posts. In 1931 a length of wharf timber dating from AD 75 was discovered on Fish Street Hill and now stands in a glass case in the church of Saint Magnus the Martyr in Lower Thames Street.

What would our early boat-dwelling venturers take on their return to Oxford? Wine, exotic foods from the Mediterranean – figs, dates, olives – as well as finer Samian pottery perhaps to be delivered to the villa-dwellers of Silchester, the large Roman settlement near the navigable River Kennet, linked to the Thames near Reading. And so after a night's rest our intrepid crew are off again, brains ablaze perhaps by the novel atmosphere of the metropolis of London. Ahead of them stretched the wild waters of the tidal Thames and beyond. It is a more difficult pull upstream, so they look forward to the quiet reaches and the level flows, the mysterious islets where a night's camp is a safer option than stopping on the main bank. The itinerant liveaboard has been born: a tribe separate from the flow of mainstream humanity, looked down on at times as coarse, unruly folk, beyond the margins of civilised society. In spite of this image, however, these first houseboat dwellers were the worker ants that kept the motor of the public and private weal running.

All over Britain river folk were living and working thus. And so the centuries passed, a thousand seasons of baleful winters and scorching summers. Generation after generation of Britons growing up in riverside settlements became apprentices to their boatmen fathers, and plied their way along the waterways until they too grew old, and taught their sons and daughters. By the time the 400 years of Roman rule came to an end, a permanent body of river-dwelling folk had grown up, and would henceforth never shrink – occasionally decimated by plague or war, but never wiped out.

And as they steered their way through the decades and the passing years, they saw the country gradually transforming. They saw towns grow up on the banks, and wharves and jetties and cities, while a hundred different types of boat slowly festooned the waterways up and down the country. London expanded to Westminster and beyond, even to the far reaches of Chelsea and Fulham, famed for their market gardens and fruit growing. And not only London: Chester, Norwich, Gloucester were cities that owed their rise to being on tidal rivers at places where they could be bridged.

Invaders came and went, Saxon kings were born and died, and out of the mist emerged an England built upon national unity, a free yeomanry, manufacture and trade. And in the common weal, it was the river populations, the boat dwellers, that were the key components of the circulatory system that kept the body politic alive.

A golden age of river dwelling had begun.

2

WHEREVER A
ಞಲ DUCK GOES ಲಞ
RIVER DWELLING AD 400–1750

Between the collapse of the Roman Empire and the beginnings of canal mania is a vast sweep of time. At its beginning Britain is an imploded, fractured island: the unity afforded by the imperial domination of the Romans has all but evaporated, trade has withered up, roads have been allowed to decay, and the tribes of mainland Europe are eyeing the vacuum with migratory relish.

It is an odd, unsettled era. Whether or not Britain truly entered a 'Dark Age' is still a matter for historians to dispute, but it is beyond question that trading patterns, and therefore the life patterns of boat dwellers, underwent some dramatic shifts and alterations.

The contrast with the end of this period, 1750, couldn't be starker. By then Britain was on the verge of being the greatest imperial power the world had ever known and the most formidable economic powerhouse in the globe. Its rivers teemed with vessels swollen with goods, and the country was about to experience nothing less than an inland waterways revolution.

After the Romans left, trade became subject to the vicissitudes of an unstable society prey to invasion, counter-invasion, war and conquest: Angles, Saxons, Jutes, Danes, Vikings – the latter even setting up camp in Fulham. The Saxons dispersed native Britons and took root, establishing the great kingdoms of Wessex and Mercia. The life of the rivermen and boat dweller was thrown into confusion; the relatively organised trade routes of the empire were replaced by tribal trade between invader and home country – for example most Danish (Viking) trade was with their home countries, proved by the prevalence of British coins found in Scandinavian regions. Whereas the river dweller would have borne allegiance to the local Roman villa, or the military, now they were in abeyance to whoever held sway over their territory at the time, whether it be Frisian or Jute.

Trade, both foreign and internal, didn't vanish; it simply adapted to the new geopolitics. From the sixth century onwards silver coins proliferated – *sceattas* – millions being in circulation in the south and east, indicating a sophisticated commerce and by definition expansion of river-borne business. From the seventh century onwards ports in England and Francia began developing, with coastal emporia, or marketplaces, many with the suffix -*wic*: Harwich, Dunwich, Sandwich – even London was known as 'Lundenwic'. The Venerable Bede described London as 'an emporium of many peoples coming from land and sea', and as we have seen, London was no longer the walled fortress of Roman times but was extending along the Strand, with huge fairs and markets in places like Covent Garden. Excavations have revealed a huge surge in boatbuilding in this period, proving that Anglo-Saxon England – despite its unsettling beginnings – was emerging as a gradually unifying nation with a growing inland river commerce.

The proliferation of the Saxon *wic* is, of course, the key motor and expression of this growth. Beginning as a largely self-sufficient settlement (the word *wic* is derived from the Latin *vicus*, or 'hamlet') the more successful wics would soon be operating on surpluses, so became trading hubs. And as aforementioned, the most successful wics were those on or near rivers – York, Southampton and, of course, London. The seamanship of the Saxons would easily have been transferred to inland navigation.

Yet throughout this gradual growth, life for the river trader and boat dweller was made difficult by a number of things, chiefly that little was being done to improve the navigability of rivers – indeed, an argument can be made that conditions worsened. It has been noted that people who worked the rivers were in competition with each other. For example, there was conflict with those who operated the fish weirs, whose structures were the bane of a river trader's life.

Worse even than the fish weirs were the mill owners. Watermills gradually became mortal enemies of the boat dwellers, who desired little more than an unhampered journey. By the time of the *Domesday Book* in 1089 there were no fewer than 10,000 mills in England – a huge impediment to navigation. John Taylor, waterman and poet, is writing in 1632, towards the end of our period, but in his lyrical *Description of Thames & Isis*, he could just as well be describing the life of a riverman in the tenth century:

> *I from Oxford down to Staines will slide,*
> *And tell the rivers wrongs which I espied.*
> *Haules Weare doth almost cross the river all,*
> *Making the passage very straight and small.*
> *How can that man be counted a good liver,*
> *That for his private use will stop a river?*

Implicit in this poetical complaint is the belief that the river does not belong – or *should not belong* – to anyone, and those who choose to live and work on it should be unimpeded by interference. This is a common theme that recurs time and again throughout this book, a persistent state of distrust and 'war' between water folk and the authorities. Even mill owners were 'landlubbers' who exploited the river but did not truly know it or respect it. It is this conflict and separation that led to river – and later, canal – dwellers to look on themselves as a distinct community and subculture. We've already noted the obstacle that fish weirs were to the free passage of traders: they were forbidden by Richard I in an article of the Great Charter, but this was evidently an ongoing war subject to periodical edict, for the frequency of complaints about fish weirs in ensuing centuries proves that the battle between navigators and fishers had not been resolved.

It is perhaps partly an illusion, then, to think a life on the river was ever totally free, for boat people were in a constant state of war with authorities. And it was not just the keepers of fishing weirs and mill owners but the operators of ordinary weirs: from the earliest times, payment was required each time a vessel passed through. The collectors of tolls at these places became hated, symbols of officialdom and civilisation intruding on the essential wildness of river life.

The difficulties of living on the river, however, were always to be trumped by the importance water transport had to the emergent medieval economy, the winning card being the relative ease and cheapness of water-borne trade compared to that of the road, and this crucial factor led to some easing of the riverman's challenges. While Roman roads, despite being neglected, were still tolerably serviceable – paving of them was maintained periodically – throughout the period, water transport, for heavy goods at

Winchester City Mill, the oldest watermill in Britain. For centuries mills were the mortal enemy of the river dweller.

Old watermills, Streatley-on-Thames. By the time of the Domesday Book in 1089 there were no fewer than 10,000 mills in England – a huge impediment to navigation.

least, remained both easier and cheaper. This assured the survival of the river dweller. As we've seen, the most important cities in the realm were London, Gloucester, Norwich and Chester – water cities all. Goods could be carried far inland by boat, using a minimum of road transport. That the value of water communications was recognised by the Middle Ages is proved by Henry II granting a charter to the boat traders of Gloucester, permitting them to travel freely along the Severn with timber, charcoal and all other merchandise, and an equivalent privilege granted to the river dwellers of Nottingham on the Trent. In 1121 Henry I converted the Fosse Dyke into a navigable canal, giving the city of Lincoln access both to the Humber and the Wash, and at the Abbey in Sawtry in Huntingdonshire the intrepid monks built a canal connecting their abode with the stone quarries at Barnack in Northamptonshire.

The River Wey. Along this waterway in 1177, barges laden with timber made the three-day journey to Essex to build Waltham Abbey.

The status of waterway trade is evinced by the fact that by the end of the twelfth century a group of customs officials had been established – admittedly a mere three men in a small boat – to oversee the economic activity of the Thames in London.

One major industrial project vividly illustrates the vital role river transport played in the medieval era: the construction of Waltham Abbey carried out by Henry II between 1177 and 1183 as part of his penance for the murder of Thomas à Becket. Timber for the Abbey came all the way from Surrey, carried on the Wey, the Thames and the River Lea, the only journey on land being from Weybridge to the Wey. The lead for the roof came from the Derbyshire Peak District, carried in 265 cartloads to Boston in Lincolnshire, then by sea and river to Essex. Caen stone – a light creamy yellow Jurassic limestone – was brought from quarries in north-western France: a favourite building material, it is found all over England in both secular and ecclesiastical architecture, and all of it moved by river.

In addition to the perennial cargoes of grain, timber and wine, what new industries did the Middle Ages engender to supply our boat dwellers with novel loads? The trade in metals of all kinds grew considerably: tin in Cornwall; and iron, which was being mined in significant quantities even before Domesday but expanded mightily thereafter, the Forest of Dean in Gloucestershire being a notable centre of production, churning out picks, shovels, axes, nails and ploughs. Military goods were a bountiful source of trade for our river dwellers – no fewer than 50,000 horseshoes were shipped to London from the West Country for Richard I's crusade. From the forest forges of the Dean to the more industrialised centres of iron-making in Kent, which developed later in the thirteenth century, iron was pre-eminent. But close behind was lead and silver, particularly at Alston Moor on the borders of Cumberland and Northumberland, and the mines of Carlisle.

The huge flowering of the Potteries in Staffordshire came in the eighteenth century with Josiah Wedgwood, but that is not to say the industry was non-existent before then, and not merely supplying local demand. On the Pipe Rolls for Staffordshire is recorded, for example, the despatch of 4,000 plates and 500 cups to the king's Christmas feast at Tewkesbury in 1604.

Even in times of political turmoil trade seemed not to be overly affected. William Malmesbury, in 1125, wrote that the London wharves were 'packed with the goods of merchants coming from all countries, and especially from Germany', adding that when there is a shortage of local supplies owing to a bad harvest, the deficiency is made up from Germany. Wool and cloth, of course, were in the premier league of British goods, woven locally by a growing body of weavers consolidated by the Guild System of training and apprenticeship, but also exported in its raw state, principally to skilled Flemish weavers in the Low Countries.

While the medieval guilds held sway in the formalising of work skills on land, what equivalence was there for the waterman? One might think that by the time of writing, 2020, the lines of the ancient dynasties who lived and worked on the waterways might have petered out. This is not so: it was in the early medieval period that the great river families took root, proving that water living and working, like toil on the land, was handed down from generation to generation. In the village of Hurley, a mile upstream from Marlow, there was a family of bargemen called Freebody recorded on documents from the thirteenth century. Today, in 2021, a Peter Freebody still owns and runs a boating business on the same spot. Whereas his ancestors might have carried Knights Templar, malt, coal and timber to and from the metropolis, the current incarnation of the Freebody dynasty builds traditional craft. Peter Ackroyd in his *Thames: Sacred River* (Chatto & Windus, 2007) also cites 'the Hobbses of Henley, the Turks of Kingston, the Cobbses of Putney, The Phelpses of Hammersmith, the Murphys of Wapping, the Coes of Barking, the Crouches of Greenhithe, the Luptons of Gravesend, the Fishers of Limehouse, and the Salters of Oxford' as families that lived and worked on the rivers for centuries. This mighty litany of ancient families reaching right back to the beginnings of recorded history is testament to the truth that before the age of 'career fluidity' in the pre-industrial and industrial ages, more often than not a family would practise the same profession for generations. The oar never fell far from the barge.

In the first part of the period under our lens, AD 400–1200, the rivers of Britain saw a flowering of a myriad types of boat appear on their glistening waters: wherries, skiffs, peter boats (fishers, after Saint Peter), lighters, barques, tilt boats, shallops, eel boats, hoys and onkers. According to Laura Wright's *Sources of London English*, 1996, in medieval times there were no fewer than twenty-eight different types of vessel traversing the rivers of this island.

For our purposes, however – the history of the long-distance boat dweller – it is the classic western barge which draws our gaze. Its forerunners are the humble log boat that expanded and with its square-cut hull and flat bottom became the sturdy long-distance workhorse of the rivers from Saxon times to the present. A statute of 1514 declared that it had 'been a laudable custom and usage tyme out of minde to use the river in Barge or Wherry-Boate'. It was said that the barge could go anywhere a duck could swim, such was its flexibility and shallow draught, even accessing the upper reaches of the hitherto difficult Thames as far as Eynsham. The western barge would be rowed but also possessed a single square sail, double sail and rudder. Those without a sail could be towed by horses, the condition of the banks permitting.

Canals proper are far ahead, but improvements to the waterways were being made in a piecemeal fashion throughout the medieval period, notably at Abingdon, when an artificial channel was dug in the 1050s to bypass a section of the Thames that was difficult to navigate. But the revolution in the accessibility and speed of water travel was, of course, the invention of the pound lock.

As its name suggests, the pound lock creates an inner chamber wherein the vessel can wait until the water level has been adjusted, ready for onward travel. Guillotine gates at both ends control the often thousands of tons of water, so of necessity had to be of sterner stuff than the often rickety flash locks.

The pound lock has various competing historical provenances. The Chinese lay claim to it with the construction in AD 984 of a lock on the West River section of the Grand Canal near Huai-yin. Built by Chiao Wei-Yoit, it actually consisted of two flash locks about 250ft apart. Although a primitive form of lock was used in Belgium as early as 1180, the first pound lock in Europe was built at Vreeswijk, Holland in 1373. Like its Chinese ancestor, it also had guillotine or up-and-down gates.

The pound lock spread quickly throughout Europe during the next century and was eventually replaced by an improved system that formed the basis of the modern lock. During the fifteenth century, Leonardo da Vinci, whilst serving the Duke of Milan as engineer, devised an improved form of pound lock whose gates formed a vee shape when closed. In 1487, da Vinci built six locks with gates of this type. These gates turned on hinges, like doors, and when closed they formed a vee shape pointing upstream, thus giving them their name of mitre gates. Leonardo realised that one great advantage of mitre gates is that they are self-sealing by the pressure of the water (since they point upstream). Also when there is a difference in water level between one side and the other, the pressure holding the gates together is at its greatest. (Whether Leonardo invented this notion spontaneously or whether he was inspired by Alberti's manual on canal construction published in 1485, in which he describes a lock with two sets of gates, is not known.)

The first pound lock in Britain didn't appear until 1564, when the citizens of Topsham near Exeter employed John Trew, an engineer, to design a short (5 mile) canal to improve access from the River Exe to the sea. A lock was built at the seaward end of the Cut, a vast edifice – 189ft long – closed upstream with a pair of mitre gates with a single gate downstream at the estuary end. Known as the Exeter Ship Canal, it lays claim to be one of the first canals to contain the earliest pound lock.

The pound lock's progress was piecemeal and faltering until the canal age proper, the flash lock persisting stubbornly as a feature of river life right up until the twentieth century. Until now, only one flash-lock winch still exists, in Eynsham, Oxfordshire.

The first lock in Britain with those all-important mitre gates at either end was built on the River Lea at Waltham Abbey at the end of the sixteenth century. Its fame spread far and wide among the river community, and indeed beyond, evinced by the fact that a notable poet, William Vallan, even penned a eulogy to it. Couched as a fanciful narrative of two river fowl journeying upriver and coming across the marvel of the modern age that was the pound lock, *A Tale of Two Swannes*, published in 1590, is a hymn to this brave new world of inland navigation:

> *Down all along through Waltham street they passe*
> *And wonder at the ruines of the Abbey,*
> *Late Supprest, the walles, the walkes, the monuments,*
> *And everie thing that there is to be seene.*
> *Among them a rare devise they see,*
> *But newly made, a waterworke: the locke*
> *Through which the boats of Ware do passe with malt.*

Helpfully, Vallan goes on to describe the new invention in technical detail:

> *This locke contains two double doores of wood,*
> *Within the same cisterne all of planke,*
> *Which only fils when boates come there to passe*
> *By opening anie of these mightie doores with sleight*
> *And strange devise.*

The novelty of this 'strange devise' was gradually to pale as pound locks began slowly to proliferate along Britain's river systems. Before the explosion of artificial waterways at the end of the eighteenth century, the emphasis of the United Kingdom – unlike continental Europe, which was

One of the oldest mitre-gate locks in Britain, at Waltham.

driving forward canal building at a furious rate from the seventeenth century onwards – was on improving river navigation.

This was a godsend to the river boatman: suddenly whole reaches of
the waterways began to open up, lengthening journeys, increasing pay and
status. By 1660 there were roughly 660 miles of navigable waterways; by
1720 that had risen to 1,160 miles. The improvements to the rivers Aire and
Calder were dramatic, fuelled by the expansion of the woollen trade in the
emerging textile towns of Leeds, Halifax, Rochdale and Wakefield. After a
survey by a 'great master of Hydraulickes' John Hadley who, according to
his colleague Ralph Thoresby, thought the Aire the 'noblest river he ever
saw not navigable' a bill was introduced to Parliament by Lord Fairfax to
make the Aire navigable from Leeds and the Calder from Wakefield.

It was a remarkable feat of early engineering: ten locks were built along a stretch of 30 miles along the Aire to Leeds to overcome a rise in water level of 68ft, and ten locks on the Calder to Wakefield. The dimensions of these locks give us a vivid picture of the boats they were accommodating, for their width and length, of course, mirrored the boats. In the case of the Aire and Calder, these were 58ft by 15ft to take the Humber sailing barges.

Similar improvements to river navigation were taking place all over Britain: on the Kennet River, where the water level fell a dramatic 138ft in a mere 20 miles, locks were built alongside the mill weirs from Newbury to the Thames – wide locks, these, for the broad London barges – and extended trade from the capital deep down into the hinterlands of Berkshire and southern England.

These changes were not without their social impact. With navigable waters extending all the time across this period, smaller bargees became threatened by the encroachment of the more powerful companies. The following story reveals there was a touch of the Wild West about the life of the early-modern boatman. When William Darvall, a barge owner operating out of Maidenhead, tried to take his boats all the way down to Newbury, he attracted the ire of local bargees. The Reading boatmen were having none of it, and subjected the unfortunate boatman to murderous threats. In a letter dated 10 July 1725 they growled:

> Mr. Darvall, wee bargemen of Reading Thought to Acquaint you before it is too late, Dam You, if y. work a bote any more to Newbury we will Kill You if ever you come any more this way. Wee was very near shooting you last time, wee went with to pistols and was not too minutes too late.

In this remarkable missive we hear the voice of the riverman from across the ages: stubborn, desperate, vindictive. The enraged bargees went on to say that if ever they saw one of Darvall's boats again at Newbury they would 'bore holes in it and sink it'. (Anthony Burton, *The Canal Pioneers*, 2017).

Crime was rife on the water. Just as the communities of folk who grew up living and working afloat felt themselves apart from the mainstream of society, so too they felt apart from its laws. Smuggling, of course, was endemic near the estuaries and coasts. On many a night in the mouths of rivers across Britain, contraband was secretly whisked from vessel to shore, across mudflats, along tributaries known only to the smuggler.

There were also bands of 'river pirates' who'd cut the mooring ropes of barges and lighters tied up at night, let them drift downstream, then make their attack. In addition to these 'night plunderers' were the opportunistic 'scuffle hunters' who'd target loads left on quaysides. Then there were the renegades, the 'double agents' who'd be in league with gangs on shore and regularly threw goods to the banks to be sold on the black market.

The River Kennet as it flows through Newbury. Improvements in the eighteenth century allowed boatmen living aboard the broad London barges to travel deep into the hinterlands of southern England.

A common grisly encounter for the river dweller would have been ducking. 'Ducking stools' peppered the nation, and by definition became a familiar sight on the waterways. At Kingston-upon-Thames a purpose-built beam extended from the central arch of the bridge, and was first used in 1572 when Mrs Downing, the wife of a 'grave maker' was dipped three times 'over hed and eres' for the crime of scolding her husband. Its last recorded use was as late as 1745, when the *Evening Post* of 27 April reported: 'last week, a woman that keeps the King's Head alehouse in Kingston, in Surrey, was ordered by the court to be ducked for scolding, and was accordingly placed in the chair and ducked in the River Thames under Kingston Bridge, in the presence of two or three thousand people.'

Places of execution were also, coincidentally or not, often located near rivers. Ancient gallows stood at Tyburn and Smithfield, both close to the eponymous Tyburn river and the Fleet, at the riverside at Dagenham, Millwall, Greenwich at 'Bugsby's Causeway' (so-called as it was perhaps tainted by a 'bug' or spirit), while the Hanging Ditch in Manchester connected the rivers Irk and Irwell. And the very name of one of London's 'lost' rivers (culverted and hidden beneath the streets) the Neckinger, near Butler's Wharf at the present Tower Bridge, is rooted in a nickname for the hangman's noose, or 'devil's neckcloth'. Whether this proximity is a descendant of our ancestors' wont to sacrifice criminals to the river gods is not known, but the prevalence of waterside execution spots would suggest as much.

The story of Henley in Oxfordshire illustrates vividly the rise of the medieval boatman, right up to the early-modern period and the coming of the canals. By the end of the fourteenth century Henley had become one of the busiest inland ports in the country. Owing to the difficulties of navigating the reaches of the Thames upstream from Henley, the town became a key hub in the transfer of goods from water to road. Bargees would take tons of grain harvested from the breadbasket of Oxfordshire to the metropolis of London, and after a week's travel would return laden with luxuries, fish and heavy goods. Even when the invention of the pound lock – installed upstream of Henley at Culham, Iffley and Sandford – the town remained prosperous, as demand for goods from London rose. Cartographer and bookseller Richard Blome wrote in 1673:

Henley ... enjoyeth a considerable trade for malting; its inhabitants (which for the most part are bargemen or watermen) gain a good livelihood by transporting of malt, wood, and other goods to London, and in return bring such commodities as they and the inhabitants of the adjacent towns have need of, at easy rates: and its market, which is on Thursdays, is very considerable for corn, especially barley; which is brought them for their great malt-trade, there being oft-times in one day sold about 300 cart-load of barley.

A common sight for the river dweller was the ducking stool, still in use here at Fordwich, Kent, in 1914.

Daniel Defoe was of similar eulogistic bent, describing Henley's 'great business ... by the trade of malt and meal and timber for London', which was shipped on 'great barges ... as the other towns do'. He goes on to list the upstream cargoes traded through Reading and presumably Henley as 'coals, salts, grocery, tobacco, oils and heavy goods'.

Henley Regatta.

A WATERMAN'S WAGER

FOR A PURSE,

Open to all 4-OAR'D Boats,

(EXCEPT LONDON WATERMEN,) ALSO,

A Punting Match,

FOR HENLEY WATERMEN,

Will be Rowed for on Friday the 25th of June, 1841.

Entries to be made with the Stewards and Committee at the Town-Hall, between the hours of 11 and 12 o'Clock the same day.

By the end of the fourteenth century Henley was already one of the busiest inland ports in the country, and one in five of its inhabitants lived and worked on the river. Its prowess as an inland trading town reached well into the late nineteenth century, as this poster from 1841 testifies, declaring a wager between working boatmen.

The hills of the Chilterns surrounding Henley were carpeted in thick beechwoods, as part of a strategic replacement of the English oak as the perennial tree of our nation. The beech quickly became a much-in-demand raw material for building. As Defoe notes, 'Chilterns towns also benefit from the export of a vast quantity of local beechwood, without which the city of London would be put to more difficulty than for anything of its kind in the nation'. As late as 1888 the painter George Dunlop Leslie, who was a familiar figure on the river in his punt, remarked in his memoirs:

> Henley still possesses a very considerable wharf frontage on the river, both above and below the bridge. Near River House there is a very considerable row of granary barns, or 'sack-hiring depots,' as they are called, which I grieve to say are shortly to be pulled down.

(G.D. Leslie, *Our River*, 1888)

Leslie marvels at the town's rich heritage of river life as he ponders the lists of deaths in the parish registers: '13th November 1560, Clement the bargeman' and, more tragically, '30th April 1611, James, a bargeman, called Sweetapple, being drowned'.

And it wasn't just Henley; the towns of Marlow, Maidenhead and Abingdon became equally prosperous from the shipping of beech and malt.

Marlow has a special place in the history of river dwelling, for like Henley its very existence is founded on the waterway, indeed, its very name – Saxon *Merlau* – derives from *drained mere*. As early as 1218 there is a record of 14,000 bundles of firewood from West Wycombe being sent downriver from Wharf Street, Marlow, and even in the late nineteenth century timber was still being transported by great western barges from the Chiltern town to the metropolis. A 1794 directory describes how '... the Thames brings goods hither from the neighbouring towns, especially great quantities of meal and malt from High Wycombe, and beech from several parts of the country', while boatmen returning upstream from London would bring back coal and other goods.

By the sixteenth century Hertfordshire, Bedfordshire, Cambridgeshire and Norfolk had become the most important malt-producing counties in

England, playing a key role in supplying the capital's expanding brewing industry. Henley fits into this pattern as Simon Townley, in his *Henley-on-Thames: Town, Trade and River* (Phillimore, 2009) notes: 'wills from the period 1530–1750 show that around 13% of the population of Henley that had named professions in their legal documents were directly associated with the river – bargemen, fishmongers, maltsters.' The fact that bargemen were able to make wills was in itself testimony to their relative prosperity: very few 'workers' in the middle ages left estates worthy of probate. As the centuries passed this percentage was to increase: Townley goes on to state that:

From earliest times, Marlow was a base for river dwellers. Here in the late nineteenth century watermen load their barges for timber bound for London.

a more detailed survey of the period 1698 to 1706, based on data from the parish registers, has concluded that over a fifth of the working population were bargemen, and over a tenth were maltsters. Another 14% were labourers, of whom some presumably loaded or unloaded barges at the Thames wharfs, helped haul vessels upstream, or worked in the maltings.

Prosperous though these Thames bargemen clearly were – boosted by the expansion of trade after 1550 with the Elizabethan sea adventurers, the discovery of the New World, the founding of the East India Company in 1600, and the forging of trading connections with overseas territories such as the burgeoning markets of Protestant northern Europe – life on the whole was tough for the boat dweller. We've seen how cut-throat and dangerous it could be from the murderous plots of the Reading bargees, and the drowning of James Sweetapple of Henley in 1611.

To supplement their incomes many boat dwellers practised sideline activities. One principal second job was the selling of herbs, or 'simples', gathered from the riverbanks. These would be sold either en route or at their destination. This fringe employment tended to mark out the river population as being 'distinct' from the land dweller, endowing them with traits more commonly associated with heathenism or witchcraft.

Amateur herbalism was not the only thing that made the rest of society regard boat people in a different light. When not living on their barges, the river dwellers usually occupied the humblest and most decrepit cottages in a town or village, and came to be looked on by residents with at best suspicion and at worst downright scorn. There is a Thameside street in Marlow – now very salubrious of course – called St Peter Street (formerly Wharf Street) whose damp, dilapidated cottages were occupied for centuries by bargees, wharfingers and brewers' labourers. Photographs from the late nineteenth century show run-down, crude dwellings that had clearly not changed for centuries.

Certainly the language and behaviour of boat dwellers distinguished them from their land-based cousins and attracted disdain. A French traveller in the eighteenth century remarked of the rivermen he encountered that, 'they use singular and quite extraordinary terms, generally very coarse and dirty ones, and I cannot possibly explain them to you'. River slang became notorious and, indeed, widely known – even the Oxford English Dictionary includes the term 'water-language' defined as 'the rough language of watermen'. While rivers remained treacherous places, and before towpaths and embankments had become ubiquitous, gangs of men would congregate at villages and trading posts, their job being to tow the boats along stretches which were dangerous or when the square-sailed barges were bereft of wind, or horses were not available. These 'hauliers', though not strictly boat folk, acquired a dreadful reputation and the river dwellers were tainted by association.

In his famous *Tour Thro' the Whole Island of Great Britain* of 1724, Defoe calculated that on any one day there were 2,000 vessels on the Thames alone. Add to this the Severn, the Trent and all the other smaller rivers taking trade deep into the heartlands right across Britain, this was a growing subculture of river-dwelling population. That Defoe chose to make note of this expansion signals its importance to the eighteenth-century observer. And as the century progressed it became more and more apparent that Britain's transport system could not keep up with the gearchange of industrial revolution. Something had to be done. And it was obvious to all that the solution didn't lie in roads.

In medieval times and beyond, right up to the seventeenth century and beyond until the growth of turnpikes, Britain's roads were still, by all accounts, dreadful, unmade, unbevelled and subject to the natural threats of flood and the man-made perils of attack from roadside thieves and highwaymen. The very nomenclature of certain names for our roadways that still persist give us an echo of the parlous conditions a traveller would encounter when travelling by horse or foot: Knaves Wood, Thieves Hollow, etc. Right up to Elizabethan times when the carriage and cart began to eclipse the packhorse, many seemed to talk of little else than the deplorable condition of the highways. Act after act was passed, all to no apparent avail. Even in his retirement Shakespeare signed a petition calling for the improvement of Warwickshire's roadways, a subject clearly dear to the heart of one who commuted regularly back and forth from his home town to the newly teeming metropolis. A statute of 1555 declared that 'highways are both very noisome and tedious to travel on, and dangerous to all passengers and carriages'. Moreover, traffic in the cities was seemingly as congested as some parts are still today. The great historian John Stowe, writing in his *Survey of London* in 1598, lamented the heaving road traffic thus:

> Ludgate in the west was in this place so crossed and stopped up that the carriage through the city westward was forced to pass south down Ave Mary Lane.

As it was for the travellers, so too for the packhorses and carting companies: road trade was the weakest link in the logistical chain from source to river to market. This meant that throughout the period 1500–1900, road transport remained much more expensive than river transport, a hard truth that paved the way for the emergence and expansion of canals as the foundation for a new era of houseboat dweller.

St Peter Street (formerly Wharf Street), Marlow, whose damp, dilapidated cottages were occupied for centuries by bargees and wharfingers while not away on the river.

Something had to be done to keep up with the increased production that was the inevitable outcome of an emergent industrial economy. If roads weren't good enough, and there weren't enough natural waterways to cope, then there was only one solution: we had to build our own.

So in a unique pocket of time – between 1770 and 1850 – the canal became the supreme form of transportation in the country. This curious window, this oasis, lay between the generally deplorable state of Britain's roads and the coming of the railways. In this brief sparkling margin, life on man-made waterways flowered, and a whole new community was born. And it is this extraordinary era to which we now turn.

3

THE CANAL AGE

1750–1900

The economic story of canals and how they fuelled the matrix of an industrial and imperial Britain has been told many times. The focus of this book is to fix a lens on the reality of day-to-day living on these growing arteries, that from the mid-eighteenth century onwards expanded the population of liveaboards to almost unimagined proportions. But to comprehend the scale of this extraordinary tectonic shift in the social history and demographics of Britain it is necessary to widen one's gaze and contemplate the broader historical context in which how, in a space of fifty years or more between 1780 and 1830, half a million people uprooted themselves and exchanged a life on the land for a life afloat.

We've seen that there had been piecemeal and pragmatic canal construction from Roman times onward – Fosse Dyke, the River Lea, the Fleet Navigation built by Robert Hooke in 1680 (surrounding street names such as Seacoal Lane and Newcastle Close bearing witness to its past as a conduit for the delivery of northern fuel to the metropolis). But there had been no national strategy. Not that there was a 'strategy' in the age of canal mania beyond the uniform acceptance that canal building was a highly profitable enterprise built firmly on a massive and growing demand. Once the Bridgewater Canal, opening in 1761, had proved itself – with its magnificent aqueduct designed by Brindley crossing the River Irwell attracting thousands of tourists – there was no stopping the tide, and private investors flocked to buy shares in their local man-made waterway. Only a few years later Britain – almost without stopping to think, and having lagged behind continental Europe for so long – had constructed the world's first national canal network.

Precisely how did the Bridgewater Canal 'prove itself'? The numbers speak for themselves. A single barge could carry 30 tons, drawn by a lone horse. This was ten times the amount that a team of packhorses could carry on land. In the first year alone, the price of coal carried to Manchester along the Bridgewater Canal fell by two thirds. Suddenly there was a huge demand for people to staff the boats, and the waterways found thousands willing to uproot themselves and take to the water.

This 'uprooting from the land' is crucial. Sonia Rolt, in her sublime book *Canal People, the Photographs of Robert Longden* (Sutton, 1997), captures the essence of the social history of canal folk. Along with hundreds of other women Rolt was recruited by the Ministry of Transport to help work the family boats throughout the inland waterway network during the 1939–45 war, in exactly the same way as land girls worked the fields:

> Many found the experience astonishing and enriching. The boat com-munity – the descendants of those families recorded during the last half the nineteenth century and perhaps earlier – had, in their lives and the structure of their community, some elements of the pre-in-dustrial, even pre-enclosure, village society. This was evidenced still in their sense of cohesion yet independence, in their self-reliance, strong loyalties, and strict family morality.

(Sonia Rolt, 1997)

So, first and foremost, where did these canal folk actually come from? It's one thing to build a canal in the late eighteenth century, another to people

The Bridgewater Canal opened in 1761, and was the birthplace of the narrowboat liveaboard. (Engraving: R. Sands, 1833)

it at whim with skilled navigators and their families capable of travelling long distances with trusted cargo. The first canals constructed were principally to connect rivers, such as the Trent and Mersey Canal, opened in 1777 under the supervision of the great engineer James Brindley. This was 93 miles of waterway, connecting two emerging industrial hubs. Simply put, how was it to be staffed?

The first answer is, of course, from the existing river traders. With an urgent and ongoing need for people capable of navigating long barges great distances, what better resource than those who had for perhaps generations plied their way along the natural waterways? Large pools of these men were to be found already local to most rivers in Britain – canals were simply an extension of their work. For centuries boatmen and their families had traversed the Thames, the Severn, the Trent, carrying cargoes that powered and fed medieval and early-modern England. When carrying companies set up post at the hubs of canals they would contract a captain and crew as necessary. At first, when canals were short – such as the Bridgewater from Worsley Mines to Manchester – they would contract daily crews, much like couriers today, but when the canal network expanded, and journeys began to take days and weeks, then to remain living locally was impossible. Thus the early-modern houseboat dweller was born. So there was an existing pool of skilled navigators to draw on, but this was finite, and so to keep up with the pace of expansion many thousands were lured from the land to a life afloat. This wasn't the entire picture, of course, and the gypsy origins of the canal folk, with particular reference to L.T.C. Rolt's findings, will be addressed later in the chapter, while H. Hanson, in his *The Canal Boatmen* of 1975, favoured the migrator from the land or indeed a small farmer combining seasonal farming work with a life afloat.

Sonia Rolt's observation on the unique world view and character of the boat dweller cannot be overemphasised; yes, the navigators were often employed and contracted, but in contrast with their land-bound cousins these were independent, solitary figures, imbued with a certain toughness, stubbornness, self-reliance and a freedom of spirit that was a direct descendant of the autonomy of the British yeoman. Once they'd set off from the industrial hub or the inland port with their cargo, they were embarking on a self-contained voyage, in obeisance to no one but their own resources, fortitude, stamina and character. It is risky to embrace any inherited cliches of national characteristics, but the heritage of Britain as a maritime nation, with its fostering of an individualism and the pioneer spirit, must inevitably have fed into the character and nature of those choosing – or, by dint of their family tradition – gravitating towards an onboard life. The masters of these early canal barges were called captains, and when you are captain of your vessel, you are to a huge extent captain of your soul.

So individuals, yes, but as canal mania gripped the nation and thousands took to a life on the water, a camaraderie evolved: a kinship, a community, almost a nation within a nation. This was a continuum of cottage industry, the nuclear family unit, the fulcrum of economic life.

While other families entered factories and apprenticeships and were fractured through migration to other towns and areas for work, boat families remained together, forging a bond that was increasingly under threat for their land-tied counterparts.

For these 'communities on the move' there were, however, many established hubs across the country where they'd meet, re-forge connections, build friendships and marry. One such locale was Braunston in Northamptonshire, which became known as the boatmen's spiritual home, with its pubs, shops and bases for loading and offloading cargo. Lying between the junction of the Oxford Canal and the Grand Union, it was ideally placed to become the boat-dweller's 'city', and for more than 150 years was the visible anchor and 'homestead' of a drifting community. Much like Crewe railway station became a meeting point for itinerant variety artistes in the late-nineteenth and first half of the twentieth centuries, Braunston was a vibrant confluence of liveaboards, the Rome of the canal system. To this day its churchyard bulges with the graves of hundreds of expired boating folk. Messages could be left for friends and relatives, knowing that they would eventually pass through; shops and pubs sprang up exclusively for canal-dwellers; and the whole effect was to create a vast subculture separate from mainstream society.

Braunston, Northamptonshire, for two centuries the hub of working canal life in England. Here a nineteenth-century family of bargees dress up for the camera.

Interior of a nineteenth-century narrowboat, nicknamed 'Monkey Boats', 1874.

It truly was a Golden Age for the British Boatman. But as the nineteenth century wore on and railways expanded to encroach on the hegemony of canals by taking over much of the national haulage, so the canal companies were forced to lower their charges, and as a consequence bargemen and their families had to live on less. This golden age of boat living – 1770–1850 – was over. Before the coming of the railways it was mainly just the men of the families who would live aboard, but as railway mania bit deep a lowering of wages and standards for the canal folk meant that to save rent whole families began to settle on the water on a permanent basis.

In 1874 a reporter for the *Illustrated London News* spent some time with a narrowboat family and published his findings on 10 October of that year. He described the boats as 'floating homes, under circumstances too often of much discomfort'. Emphasising that these communities were 'not gypsies', the tenor of his piece firmly places the liveaboard communities of the canals as socially and morally superior to their caravan-dwelling counterparts. An article of its time indeed, with the prejudices of its age, yet there is a certain accuracy in its reflection of the social respect afforded to canal dwellers. Often these were employees, for example, of noteworthy and highly respected companies – Pickfords, Fellows, Mortons and Claytons were giants of Victorian industry, powerhouses of the nation's prosperity. Boat dwellers might be itinerant but they were, palpably and visibly, not wastrels or 'undeserving poor'.

The article in the *Illustrated London News* goes on, with the help of engravings, to depict the house-proud – or boat-proud – nature of the canal families in their elaborate decorations of their dwellings, art which we know to be akin to that of the Romanies – baroque, intricate, floral. Its iconography is still ubiquitous on the waterways, handed down through the years by dedicated traditionalists. It is probably not a coincidence that what has become known as traditional 'narrowboat art', with its classic iconography such as Roses and Castles, began when women started to live aboard in the second half of the nineteenth century.

Roses and castles, for centuries the iconic decorative art of the canal boat, suggested by some to be an archaic memory of the fairy-tale fortresses of Eastern Europe from whence the first canal people came. (Robert Longden)

We know the Victorian age to be one of high contrasts: as industrial civilisation tightened its grip and expanded its tendrils across the nation there flowered a reactive sentimentality for pre-urban life, and boat dwelling and working fell into the orbit of that yearning. With its open-air existence and strong hint of carefree vagabondage some Victorians painted a rustic picture of boat life akin to the Elizabethan poets' eulogies to shepherds of the 1500s: pastoral, romantic, free from the cares of grinding everyday toil in the cities and towns.

There is a danger in falling prey to this poetic vision. Whilst there were evident joys and freedoms to be gleaned from a life on the water in the era of canal mania, we must beware this portrayal of it as a semi-rustic idyll. Not merely hard-headed realism but cold research tells us that disease and hardship were as rife on these houseboats as they were in city tenements. In the relatively rustic town of Braunston in the 1830s there were seventy cases of cholera, and nineteen deaths. Sanitation on board the narrowboat was virtually non-existent, and the waters of the canals were soon rapidly poisoned, not merely with the industrial effluent dumped by bankside factories but also human waste from the families on board. Almost every canal in the country became un-swimmable. As house-proud as the liveaboards were, with facilities on board being so cramped – the average cabin on a barge was 7ft by 5ft – there is a limit as to how clean one can keep one's abode.

So the other side of the coin to the depiction of boat life as liberating and contributory to a life of self-reliance, is one of suffering, injury, disease and hardship, particularly for children.

The major documentary historian of life on houseboats in the nineteenth century is George Smith, one of those extraordinary Victorian campaigners for the improvement of ordinary people's lives, worthy of being ranked alongside Dickens, Mayhew and Shaftesbury. Smith published the magnificent *Our Canal Population* in 1875, and it paints a wildly opposing picture of boat life to our slightly fey, dreamy journalist from the *Illustrated London News* who appeared mesmerised by the beautiful artwork and boaters in their Sunday best. He followed this up with *Gypsy Life* in 1880, hinting at his strong belief that the water-dwelling population and the caravan dwellers were akin. ❧

Himself a child labourer – he had carried clay for thirteen hours a day in a brickyard at Coalville, Leicestershire, from the age of 7 – Smith had a personal axe to grind, much like Dickens whose life was traumatised by being forced into a bottle-labelling factory in London at a similar age. A volley of furious letters to newspapers bewailing the lack of access to schooling and religion on the part of canal folk ('Of the children of these 100,000 boatmen not more, probably, than 2,000 will be found to attend either day school or Sunday School') was followed by extensive explorations into the world of canal life crystallised in his magnum opus *Our Canal Population*. The picture Smith painted was not a golden one. Having campaigned to improve the conditions of children working in the Leicestershire potteries and brickworks, Smith now focused his coruscating gaze on the water folk, and found them wanting. His work led to the Canal Boat Act of 1877 and the Prevention of Cruelty to Children Act – known as the Children's Charter – of 1889, which cemented in law the requirement to register the number of those living aboard and necessitated regular inspections of sanitary conditions and a report on school attendance. Noble though Smith's work was – having seen the deplorable conditions in factories he considered it 'monstrous that with the Factory and Workshop Act of 1871, passed and in activity, it should be possible to have women and children herding together and employed as in these boats, so the Education Act should be inoperable in relation to these boatmen's children' – his missionary zeal was not entirely free from a certain Victorian moralising. 'His purely animal life,' he wrote of the boatman in *Our Canal Population*, 'devoid of all spiritual and almost all social influences, has produced in him a low and coarse animalism', a judgement steeped, one cannot help but infer, in a social snobbery that extends beyond mere concern for the physical well-being of his subjects.

For many the social reforming zeal of the late Victorians towards the boat people was looked on as a shining example of the better angels of our nature, but not everyone saw it that way. For many boat people, George Smith the campaigner represented someone merely 'sticking his nose in' their affairs. He compiled data for his magnum opus from numerous interviews with canal folk, and on many occasions if they saw him approaching on the tow-path they'd let slip the ropes and simply flee, instructing their children not to talk to the sociological busybody. This instinct to spurn the attentions of officialdom, more than anything, is evidence of the essential 'outsiderishness' of the houseboat dweller, of being apart from the mainstream of 'normal' society, beyond the nets of its laws, customs and diktats.

In his book Smith complains of liveaboard women washing over the sides of the boats topless: this, surely, is more than concern for the conditions of his fellow human beings but a superior judgement superfluous to his primary aim, and betrays a special pleading deeply rooted, no doubt, in his religious impulses. Smith's was not only a crusade for well-being but also a push against a growing cultural trend towards romanticising boat life, in the same way as the caravan life of itinerant Romanies had been beautified in the imagination by artists and writers of the late nineteenth century, such as authors like George Borrow, whose *Lavengro* and *Romany Rye* presented the wayfaring world of gypsies as an idyllic existence rather than a life of travail to be pitied and reformed.

Smith's view of the boat dweller was possibly more realistic than the dewy-eyed versions of the romantic writers – whose idealisation of water life was akin to the Elizabethans' sanitised elevation of the humble shepherd to the status of a 'noble savage' – but nevertheless there were counterbalances to his harsh portrayal. Author and campaigner Henry Mayhew, writing earlier than Smith in 1851, interviewed many boatmen for his famous *London Labour & London Poor*, and though not diluting the hard nature of the work, had praise at least for their sobriety, remarking quite convincingly that 'a drunken lighterman, I was told, would hardly be trusted twice'. In London at least the boat people experienced sophisticated levels of employment:

> The Trinity Company, whom I serve [divulged a boatman to Mayhew] and have served for thirty years, are excellent masters to us when we are sick … The corporation of the Trinity House allow the married lightermen in their service 10s, and the single ones 7/6d a week as long as they are ill. I have known the allowance given to men for two years, and for this we pay nothing to any benefit society or provident fund.

(Henry Mayhew, 1851)

Inside a classic Romany caravan – the origin of the narrowboat interior?

Certainly not every carrying company treated its boatmen and their families as benevolently as the Trinity Corporation, but there was nevertheless a living to be made; and perhaps the occasional instability and financial uncertainty (will there be a load back when I get to London?) was a price the boatman was willing to pay for being, almost, his own boss. No factory foreman shouting at you above the noise of the milling machines, no fixed hours, just up at dawn, and the breeze in your hair as you steered your 30 tons down the Cut, passing the warehouses and the factory yards and the mills and gliding out into the wide-open green embrace of the countryside.

By the second half of the nineteenth century, then, the phenomenon of the permanent floating family was a fact sufficiently widely known as to attract the attention of social campaigners such as Smith. The church too began to fix its lens on the canal folk. Just as missionaries would venture deep into foreign lands in order to nourish the moral life of those inhabitants they found there who, in their eyes, lived beyond the margins of true 'civilisation' so too the floating population of river folk lived outside the boundaries of normal society. To mainstream society houseboat dwellers were therefore in danger of losing their grip on morality, ethics and the teachings of the church.

The solution? Floating churches. Smith's views on boat dwellers as straying into the dangerous territory beyond the reach of the teachings of Christianity filtered into the common realm, particularly fiction. The authoress L.T. Meade – famous in her day – wrote around 200 books, published mainly by church organisations, the principal themes of which were that the lack of education amongst boat people led to their ignorance of religion and inability to reach salvation. Meade describes boat people as being 'a race apart'. In her novel *Water Gipsies,* an Aunt asks her niece on her deathbed, 'what is Jesus?' For late Victorian moralists, such as Meade, if you lived outside the clutches of a town or village, then your soul too dwelt outside in the 'wilderness', and it is of course the job of a moralist to save you. Other books, such as *Dick of the Paradise* by Alfred Colbeck, and *Rob Rat: A Story of Barge Life* by Mark Guy Pearse, echo this perception.

Thus the floating chapels were born: first, missionaries put up tents at transport hubs such as Braunston in Northamptonshire, but soon services began to be held on board special ecclesiastical vessels. These weren't very different to the Seamen's Missions that had existed for decades. Some of these canal chapels were semi-permanent structures, thrown up on the banks, but many were actual boats – sixty, in fact, roaming the inland waterways in search of the devout. This mission to succour the spiritual needs of boat dwellers had actually begun as early as 1844. The Weaver Churches Bill of that year asked that Christian teaching be made compulsory for those living afloat. The petitioners asserted their claims thus:

On the broader canals at least, a condemned barge, *vulgo* a flat, may be converted at trifling expense into a floating chapel, suitable for a congregation of 150 adults. We can bear witness that such have been filled by zealous and grateful worshippers, many of whom had never before with holy bell been tolled to church. We think that the sternest opponents of cheap churches, the greatest sticklers for spires, chancels and rood lofts, would forego his objections in favour of these arks of refuge, if he could witness their effects.

Some of these floating temples were successful, others not so. The Boatman's Chapel in Oxford, a converted barge moored up at Castle Stream, which provided a Sunday school for up to 100 pupils, quietly sank one morning in 1868 – an outcome, as one contemporary account put it, of 'being possessed of less endurance than the Vicar, and probably weary and disgusted with its poor surroundings', the writer adding ruefully, 'It was not worth raising.'

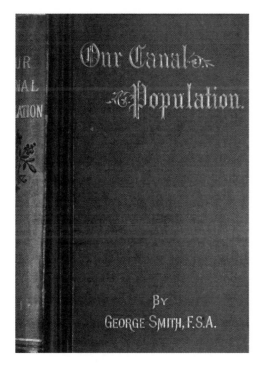

George Smith's *Our Canal Population* of 1874 is perhaps the most important study of life on the inland waterways of the nineteenth century.

Mixed though the fortunes of these floating churches were, their descendants persist to this day, though in slenderer numbers: The Boater's Christian Fellowship was formed in 1995, and since 2004 a converted Dutch barge operates as St Peter's Barge in West India Quay in London.

As we have seen, the moral crusade to treat the souls of boat dwellers was matched by the desire to help them physically in terms of living and working conditions, and canal people can owe George Smith a huge debt for both the Canal Boat Act of 1877 and the Prevention of Cruelty to Children Act, or Children's Charter, of 1889.

It's fair to say that day-to-day life for the working boat dweller in the period 1750 to 1900 wasn't that different to the river traders of earlier times. Certainly the manpower required for inland navigation remained largely unchanged: the bargeman who was 'captain' – sometimes the merchant as well as the carrier – crew members, either hired labour or business partners, and bow hauliers engaged to tow the barge. As time went on these patterns would vary. Some hauliers were not liveaboards and would be recruited as local gangs from the area through which the boat was travelling, and many barges became horse drawn as the nineteenth century progressed and towpaths improved. As we have seen, with the coming of the railways when there was downward pressure on a boatman's wages, whole families would live aboard to save money, and act as labour, so the number of hired crew fell, though to maximise income many families would drive two barges.

Whilst acquiring a reputation as being tough and vulgar, the boatman and his family were nevertheless a highly skilled workforce. Given the interconnectedness of the canal network with the rivers, it is often forgotten that most canal bargees also had to possess an advanced knowledge of navigating tidal estuaries, which posed unique challenges. Estuaries were prone to sudden sharp changes in level as L.T.C. Rolt notes in his *The Inland Waterways of England* (Allen & Unwin, 1950):

> ...while the Vale of Gloucester lay basking in sunshine a great storm might be raging over the mountains around Plynlimmon (sic) to send a roaring spate of flood water down the Severn and her tributary Vyrnwy which might cause the river to rise as much as 18ft in five hours at Gloucester and so entirely alter conditions in the estuary below.

The skill involved in navigating treacherous waters while carrying a valuable and heavy cargo cannot be exaggerated: the boatman would have to make split-second decisions as to whether he was able to manoeuvre his vessel over a weir without the use of a lock, or maintain a certain course in a flooded reach. Pools, shallows, islets, islands, eyots – many of which might be transient features – were given names by the navigators that only later found their way onto maps. This knowledge was handed down from father to son, and to entire families in the latter part of the nineteenth century.

In times of winter floods the landscapes around rivers would be altered beyond recognition to anyone not familiar with their seasonally hidden contours. The skilled boatman would have to steer a course in the main current by means of landmarks – a church steeple, a tree on higher land. While there was some overlap between the riverman and the canal man, distinctions there were, in both skills and language: river traders by and large adopted the terminology of the seagoer – port, starboard, warps, hatches, etc. – which for the canal bargee became 'outside' or 'inside' depending on the position of the towing path, and hatches are 'slides' and warps 'lines'. As canals became the dominant inland waterway, bargees became fiercely protective of their skills and lore, despite it being dismissed by seagoing sailors as mere 'ditch crawling'. This was a woeful underestimate of the skill involved, evinced by the case of a group of ex-merchant seamen taking to the boats of the Grand Union Canal. After discovering that the work involved in taking a boat from Birmingham to London was more onerous than they'd envisaged, one crew deserted as they were about to enter Braunston tunnel, and made off over the fields. Luckily their unmanned vessel, drifting like a canal version of the *Marie Celeste*, was rescued by an oncoming pair of Fellows Morton boats coming in the opposite direction.

We've seen that in the earliest days of canals the existing river population was drawn on to man the new waterways, but this cannot be the whole picture. L.T.C. Rolt, one of the great pioneers of canal history, has done extensive research into the possible gypsy origins of the liveaboard communities spawned by the canal era, and has concluded that the Romany culture and that of the river and canal dweller is inextricably linked. The very first canal constructed by James Brindley, the famous Bridgewater, crossed Trafford Moss at Manchester, which was a noted haunt of gypsies, and in the late eighteenth century, when canal mania took off, there was a large body of Romanies recently migrated from the Balkans. Rolt concludes that not only must their labour have been utilised in construction but also in manning the boats when the Cut was completed. Since then the growing canal population was swelled by non-Romanies but the beginnings of the phenomenon of houseboat living in the canal age was fundamentally gypsy. Canal boats required not so much navigational skills as a way with horses, which of course Romanies excelled in, and there was not much contrast between life in a horse-drawn wagon and life aboard a horse-drawn boat.

It is clear that the very layout, 'body plan' and design of the canal barge is an echo of the Romany caravan: the stern end corresponds to the wagon's driving-platform; the coal range is traditionally on the left in both the caravan and barge; the 'side-bed' acting as both seat and bed occurs in both; the fold-down crockery cupboard creating a table; and a preponderance of linen and lace curtains and fashioned metal pots and pans make the narrowboat almost a perfect floating version of the gypsy caravan.

There was a kinship and prosperity on the canals that George Smith perhaps neglected in decrying canal folk as being little better than uneducated vagabonds.

There was no seagoing equivalent of the narrowboat, in either design or function, except maybe the Danish longboat, and clearly it counted the western river barge amongst its ancestors, but as a place of family habitation – chiefly a phenomenon of the canal age – Rolt concludes that the progenitor has to be the gypsy caravan. Brass rails, ornamental plates and copperware all point to a cultural link with the folk art of nomadic people, as does the decorative paintwork with its traditional iconography of roses, castles and so on. Because this embellishment of canal boats blossomed in the second half of the nineteenth century though, when more and more women began to live aboard, the connection with purely Romany origins is tricky to prove, chiefly because in the pre-photographic age there are scarcely any images of narrowboats apart from engravings, which do not show decorations. Rolt, however, is of the conviction that the iconographic similarities alone demonstrate a symbiosis, especially with the ubiquitous castle, which Rolt asserts derives from folk memory of the gothic fortresses of Eastern Europe. So with music: the mutual love of step dancing and music points to an affinity quite probably based on blood and inheritance.

The names of many of the great canal families are also Romany families: the Stanleys, Taylors, Lees and Boswells. As with many subcultures, there was much inter-marrying within the community, boat dwellers being wary of marrying 'off the land'. This was founded less on blind tradition than on plain common sense, as it would be a task indeed to persuade a woman to give up solid ground and embrace the life of an aquatic nomad. As late as 1950, when L.T.C. Rolt was researching his book on canals, he found in speaking to old narrowboaters that not only did they all know each other but professed to being related to almost everyone. This I can testify as being a common trait amongst Romanies. As a youth I spoke to the inhabitants of a traditional gypsy camp who'd set up in the meadows above the village of Temple just outside Marlow. On showing them a book of photographs of Edwardian Romanies, they recognised every one, naming them as grandfather, uncle, great-aunt, etc.

Rolt's theory is not universally accepted and is the subject of critique by waterways historian Harry Hanson who imputes a certain romantic fancy to the notion of the Romany origin of the canal dwellers. In the Register of Boats and Barges for Lancashire, Cheshire, Staffordshire, Warwickshire,

Gloucestershire, Derbyshire and Leicestershire – a stipulation from an Act of 1795 – Hanson cites, 'the names of 898 masters of boats are registered, of which 103 may be described as gypsy names.' (*The Canal Boatmen 1760–1914*, Manchester University Press, 1975). While conceding that the predilection for tin, copper and brassware demonstrates an aesthetic and occupational link with Romanies, Hanson concludes that the origins of the boat-dwelling population of the nineteenth century can't have had a single source, and this is probably the most accurate summation. Where broad canals were extensions of existing navigable rivers, especially in the north, there can be little doubt that existing owners of river craft and coastal vessels simply extended their work life onto the man-made waterways. The Sankey Canal, opened in 1757, was built to accommodate the already existent Mersey flats – broad vessels constructed for heavy goods like coal and salt – so the transition from river trader to canal trader was seamless, and in southern England the ancient boat dwellers of the Severn could navigate inland to Brimscombe via the Thames and Severn canal by 1785.

The Shropshire Union Canal, known in canal slang as 'Sloppy Cut'.

It is fair to say, then, that 'canal folk' were a delightful admixture drawn from many sources: migrators from the land looking for independence and a more reliable living, ex-miners who built the waterways then sailed on them, river traders who seized on the opportunity canals afforded to expand their horizons, small farmers who combined a seasonal life on the land with long trips afloat with their surpluses (a multiplicity of occupations was very common in the eighteenth century and indeed the 1795 Boat Register records a case of 'a number of hogs belonging to Henry Round being washed in the canal at Oldbury') and Romanies who made the effortless sidestep from wagon to floating cabin. As with all communities, however, whatever one's origin a collective identity evolves, which as the decades pass has the tendency to mislead the historian and observer into inferring a single lineage.

Certainly by the end of the nineteenth century the boat dwellers on Britain's canals were viewed as one identifiable, united community. The people of the 'cut' (it was never referred to as a 'canal' – indicating an old desire to distinguish it from the natural river) shared a common slang for a start. Narrowboats were 'monkey boats', a 'butty boat' was a second boat usually towed along behind carrying a second cargo, a practice deriving from some carrying companies' stipulation that families steer two boats to save water. There were fly boats, day boats, longboats and Rodney boats. Boats on canals never 'sailed' but 'swam'. A family that owned their own boats were 'number ones' and those who just used their craft for the day were given the derogatory appellation 'Joey boats'. Mispronunciation fed the argot of the water folk: so the Shropshire Union Canal became the 'Sloppy Cut' from Salop, Birmingham was 'Brummagam' and Walsall was 'the Ganzees'. This was the language of illiteracy, derived from a cursory phonetic glazing of signs, to be handed down through generations.

The coarseness of the boat dwellers' speech has a long tradition. Even Pepys records a savoury encounter of 4 May 1669: 'By water with my brother as high as Fulham, talking and singing and playing the rogue with the Western bargemen about the women of Woolwich.' A certain frisson existed between those on the land and the river or canal dweller, an attitude built on suspicion and distrust of those living a 'different kind of life'. Thus there were many cases of fights and all sorts between the canal folk and the people on the banks they passed. In a case that went to court, one bargeman who had a run-in with boys on the banks, complained bitterly of the lot of the boat dweller: 'Blackguard boys wot calls yer names and throws stones at yer … Then, if yer complains they pelts yer with brickbats wuss n' ever and the hull country and the magistrates sides with 'em.'

The look of the canal dweller was certainly distinct, and persisted even into the twentieth century: red or brown waistcoat with fustian sleeves, smock frocks, fur cape with side flaps and mighty hobnail boots. These boots were designed specifically for the tough life of the boatman, particularly for the 'legging' through the long tunnels, an arduous process involving lying on 'wings' perpendicular to the prow and stern and manoeuvring the vessel along, inch by inch. Proof that the discourse of canal folk was not solely unsavoury or combative is that they were known for their singing as they legged their way through these dark echoing passageways.

In his voyage to Birmingham on Captain Randle's barge for *Household Words*, Charles Dickens' magazine, in 1858, John Hollingshead waxed lyrical about this hardy footwear:

> A bargeman's boot looks more as if it had been turned out of a black-smith's forge, than a shoe-maker's stall … with upper leather as thick as a moderate slice of bread and butter. The sole bristles with a plan-tation of gooseberry-headed hob-nails. Twelve shillings a pair is paid for to makers who reside upon the canal banks, for these boots.
>
> ('On the Canal: a Narrative of a Voyage from London to Birmingham', *Household Words*, 1858)

Because of the very particular clothing needs of the canal folk, specialist tailors would spring up on the banks. William Edwards was one of this growing swathe of small businessmen who prospered as an ancillary trade. In the late nineteenth century he appealed to the Grand Junction Canal committee to open a second shop: 'I am by trade a tailor,' he declaimed, 'and have a small shop beside the canal at Braunston where I make garments for the boatmen working on the canal, but latterly many of my customers work on the Grand Union Canal.' The committee heartily approved of Mr Edwards' ambition, and gave him permission to open another shop at Buckby top lock.

Above left: A boatman on the Trent and Mersey Canal, 1890. The garb of a bargee scarcely changed throughout the history of canals – fustian waistcoat, leather trousers, tough boots.

Above right: Looking closer at the boatwoman on p.78, a typical canal-woman's garb, complete with heavy black bonnet.

The women of the canals were as sartorially distinctive as the men, the most dramatic garment being the huge bonnet shaped like a quilted cowl, forming a sheltering tunnel over her whole face. It was truly a piece of headgear built to protect the wearer from all weathers and one that persisted well into the twentieth century.

What was the financial situation of the nineteenth-century working liveaboards? It veered wildly, was precarious, and most definitely showed a slow and inexorable decline with the rise of the railways and the improvements of roads. We've seen that as the century progressed whole families began living and working aboard primarily to save money. The fierce campaigning by zealous philanthropists such as George Smith, whilst having a special missionary agenda, must have had some basis in genuine deprivation. The prosperity of the boatman depended on whether he was master or carrier: if master, then he was the only one paid and had to distribute his earnings to his crew members. Income also depended on tonnage, and whether the vessel was given a return load. Often life was more precarious for the master-owner than for the contracted carrier, for if one was employed by one of the big carrying companies – such as Pickfords, one of the great logistics firms that still operate today, though now on the roads – one would have insurance, regular work and what amounted to a salary. In many professions, such is the rate of change, there is a tendency to reminisce fondly of 'better times' and boat life was no different. In the twentieth century canal workers would hark back to the 'golden age' before road transport became supreme, and in the late nineteenth century they'd be musing mournfully on the good fortunes of their fathers and grandfathers, who enjoyed a 'bountiful life' on the waters free from the competition of the railways.

Certainly the big carrying companies from the outset held out the prospect of steady, reliable work on the waterways: an advert in the *Birmingham Gazette* of 1798 reads: 'Men of approved character wanted who will engage to steer themselves anywhere may meet with constant employment by applying to Rock, Walkers & Rock's ...' This was, of course, in the first flush of canal mania, and it is to be inferred from adverts such as these that as demand for labour was high, so too were wages. The extraordinary pace of canal construction in these first few decades was of course matched by an equal surge in demand for bargees: in 1760 there were 1,760 miles of navigable waterways in Britain (including rivers), but by 1840 this figure had risen to 4,003. A rapidly growing export trade as Britain's empire expanded was also an overarching pressure on canal growth.

The income of boat dwellers varied across the decades, and downward pressure was, of course, exerted with the coming of the railways in the period 1840–70, but as a general rule bargees and their families were quite well paid compared to other sectors of the working population. From the cash books of the Birmingham Canal Company of 1770–72 we learn that Job Lloyd earned £33 9s between 4 May and 7 September 1771 – about £6,000 at today's rates and purchasing power. Not a fortune, then, but not poverty wages, though it must be remembered that out of this Mr Lloyd would almost certainly have to pay for the horse and for an on-board assistant. It seems that wages varied according to the loads carried, for from the same registers we learn that a James Jukes earned a formidable £25 16s 6d in a single week between 5 October and 23 November 1771 carrying bricks from Birmingham to London – an impressive £2,000 at 2020 rates. The clearly hard-working widow Hannah Hipkiss earned £177 in the year 1778 for carrying coal from Wednesbury and Tipton to Birmingham – a satisfying £14,750 in 2021 terms. The Widow Hipkiss, who lived next door to the Navigation Inn, Paradise Street on the wharf at Birmingham, was evidently made of strong stuff, for she appears again in the cash register of 1795 steering a barge of coal from Tipton to Oxford, after which her sons took over the business and she presumably had a rest. In addition to these wages, bargees were also paid for extra services such as ice-breaking, and other sundry labour like unloading, and 'getting clay' (digging).

A grislier form of 'houseboat' during this time – the mid-eighteenth century to the mid-nineteenth – was, of course, the prison ship. These ghastly hulking vessels straddled the Thames from 1776 onwards, and gained reputations as floating infernos. The last one was indeed destroyed in an inferno, being set on fire in 1857, and along with its neighbours housed thousands of convicts across the decades who spent the remainder of their lives aboard the hellholes. As a result of the American War of Independence transportation of felons to this colony was no longer an option, which led to the proliferation of wooden fortresses along the Thames – the *Discovery*, the *Belliquex* and the aptly named *Retribution*, moored at Deptford, Woolwich and Chatham. Many prisoners only saw the light of day when let out for labour on shore, building docks and so on, returning at night to languish in chains. One prisoner noted the 'horrible effects arising from the continual rattling of chains, the filth and the vermin', adding that 'of all the shocking scenes I had ever beheld, this was the most distressing … nothing short of a descent to the infernal reaches can be at all worthy of a comparison with it.' On death, the convicts were unceremoniously thrown into the marshes of Plumstead, where grows a red nettle known as 'The Convict's Flower'.

The most gruesome form of 'houseboat' was the prison ship, like *Discovery* at Deptford.

The coming of the railways was not the only pressure on the canals. The disruption of the Napoleonic Wars from 1790 to 1815 temporarily disturbed shipping routes for the export market but does not seem to have inflicted any significant wounding blows on the inland waterways, given the unbroken expansion of the canals during the period. One huge pressure, however, was the increasing demand for speed: more and more merchants began insisting on quicker transport times, especially for perishable or luxury items. This led to the introduction and widespread use of the 'fly boat' – effectively a narrowboat smaller and lighter than the classic western barge that could travel at 3mph all day and night, with no mooring or stoppages of any kind, worked by four men and drawn by a relay of horses and carrying on average 15 tons as opposed to 40 tons. By 1840 fly boats were operating throughout the canal system between the inland cities and the ports. Such was their prevalence that the carrying firm Pickfords became a wholly fly-boat company.

The growth of the fly-boat trade had a marked effect on the life of the canal dweller. Men were expected to undertake longer journeys so be away from home for far longer. A Select Committee report of 1841 judged that: 'Working on the fly-boats [is a] most harassing and wretched mode of life: their Night and Day, travelling in the way in which they do, must be exceedingly wretched.' In the *Canal Boatmen's Magazine* of February 1832 a missionary bemoans that these bargees 'are little more than slaves; they toil and work day and night, week and Sunday'. As for sustenance for these round-the-clock boatmen, the missionary supplies a vignette of their comestibles: 'they arrive with their boats in London, and unload them; then re-load, obtain what drink they well can, lay in their stock of meat and peck loaves, and off.' Dickens' friend John Hollingshead in his aforementioned voyage on Captain Randle's boat from London to Birmingham in 1858 echoes this sketch of their eating habits: 'a sack of potatoes, a quantity of inferior tea, and about fifty pounds of meat at the beginning of the voyage: while large loaves of bread, weighing upwards of eight pounds, [can be] got at certain places on the line of canal.'

Fly boats were made for speed: here in 1944 a father and son carry fruit pulp along the Regent's Canal in London to the Midlands.

The required speed of delivery of these fly boats was an added pressure on the canal folk: simply put, the date of departure was stamped on the captain's passage bill and if goods were not despatched by the due date, fines were imposed which naturally impinged on the boater's income. Rivalry between the fast twenty-four-hour fly boats and the ordinary 'slow boats' was rife, particularly at points of contact such as locks. Fly boats were supposed to be permitted to queue jump at these junctions, but a practice grew of the 'slow boaters' demanding money to be overtaken, a situation that understandably led to more than a few contretemps.

We have seen that these canal folk came from a variety of backgrounds – former and continuing river traders, Romanies from the Midlands, small farmers-turned-boatmen – but they all seem to have been united by what Arthur Redford, in his *Labour Migration in England, 1800–1850* (The Economic Journal, Volume 37, Issue 148, 1 September 1927), described as the spirit of 'birds of passage, beating northwards in the springtime, in whom had awoken a vague discontent with the routine of settled life, and a longing to venture forth in quest of happier sur-roundings'. Whilst being a somewhat romantic perception, Redford's conclusion was not far from the mark. In addition to the more indus-trious and 'honest' elements of the population, there's no doubt that a floating life also attracted those who existed on the margins of society, people infused with the spirit of the vagabond. A certain 'J.C.' who'd worked on the fly boats for fourteen years confessed to a Parliamentary Commissioner's Report in 1839 that before taking to a life on the boats he'd 'spent [his] time ... lurking in fields where game lay, sometime sin beer-shops, public houses, and bawdy houses. When not in honest employ I was maintained by poaching and stealing.'

Charles Dickens had a surprisingly unromantic view of canal life. Like his friend and fellow writer John Hollingshead, whose *Canal Journey* of 1858 we have noted, Dickens made several trips on canals, seeking material for his magazine *Household Words*, on one memorable journey encountering his distant cousin William Dickens, whose father ran the Admiral Nelson Inn at Braunston on the Grand Union. Dickens' active temperament palled at the seeming slow pace of life on the waterways:

And here they were, no doubt, and here they lived from day to day, and from night to night; and a pretty wretched, dirty, monotonous life it was. Having once got into a canal, with the horse at his long tug, the tediousness of the time was not easily to be surpassed. From canal to river, and from river to canal, there was scarcely any variety, except in the passage through the locks, the management of the rope in passing another barge-horse on the tow-path, and the means to be employed in taking the horse over a bridge. The duty of driving the horse along the tow-path, as may be conjectured, fell to the lot of our young tourist. Once or twice, 'concealed by the murky shades of night,' as a certain novelist would express it, he had ventured to mount the horse's back; but the animal, not relishing this addition to his work, always took care, when they passed under a bridge, or near a wall, or hard embankment, to scrape his rider's leg along the side, so that very little good was got in that way.

(*Household Words*, 13 April 1850, p.93).

Peggotty's houseboat in *David Copperfield* is perhaps the most famous houseboat in fiction. Standing on Yarmouth sands close to the sea, the upturned fishing vessel with its two floors and cottage chimney has been variously ascribed to several existent houseboats, either at Great Yarmouth itself – though not in as close proximity to the waves as Dickens depicted in the book (probably to make its destruction by storm more believable), or a similar houseboat on the shore at Gravesend, which Dickens had seen in his twenties.

It is a point of dispute amongst historians as to how many entire families lived aboard their boats and how many also possessed homes ashore and thus divided their working life between the two. The previously accepted picture is that wives and children only began living aboard in the latter part of the nineteenth century when railway hegemony effected a downward pressure on wages, but as early as 1841 in a Select Committee on Sunday trading, Richard Heath of Stourport reported that: 'Slow boats ... carrying mineral products, where dispatch is of little consequence, then the man's wife and family often live with them.' In the same investigation a Mr Bouverie of the Grand Junction Canal Company asserted with the confidence of an insider:

Perhaps the most famous houseboat in literature, Peggotty's boat in Dickens' *David Copperfield*.

Dickens probably based Peggotty's houseboat on a similar dwelling he'd seen near Gravesend: 'a quaint little cottage consisting of an inverted fishing-boat, or navy cutter, supported upon low walls of brickwork. The entire boat, which is 30 feet long, 7½ feet beam and 5 feet deep, was used to form the roof and upper part of the house.'

a great many of the Men who navigate on the Canals have no Homes of
their own: they have no Homes but their Boats. It is the case with many
People engaged in the Coal Trade ... they carry themselves, their wives
and their Children with them.

The truth is that there were a variety of reasons why some whole families
took to the waterways and other boats were solely manned by the father.
It was noted ruefully in the same Select Committee Report of 1841 that
some wives had heard it was 'not an uncommon Thing for men to hire
females to accompany them on voyages say from London to Manchester',
so 'often times the wife goes up with her husband as a sort of Protectress'.
Other families chose to sleep at times in lodgings. The 1851 records that
the home of cordwainer and grocer Thomas Langley in Alrewas, in addition to his own family, housed 64-year-old boatman William Cox, his wife
Nancy, same age, and their servant William Winfield, 16.

As the decades passed and recruitment to the canal population became
increasingly internal (i.e. from within its ranks) the folk of the waterways
began to form a society within a society, separate from their land-bound
counterparts. This, as we have seen, aroused the suspicion of the moral
arbiters of officialdom, with campaigners like George Smith embarking
on their moral crusades. However, a more balanced view must be taken
of the 'moral state' of boat dwellers throughout the century and beyond:
certainly there was violence, and immorality, and lack of education, but it
would be a gross distortion to assert that there was any more criminality
amongst people afloat than those based on land. Certainly the financial
status of houseboat dwellers was generally greater than many urban industrial workers, if that can be used as a measure of moral condition, which
is of course doubtful. Birmingham steerers in 1839 were earning £4 10s
for a six-day week – £300 in 2020 terms, and fly-boat captains were similarly (relatively) prosperous, receiving £8 for a voyage from Manchester to
London, the equivalent of £700 – out of which, of course, they had to pay
for horses and hired labour. There are many cases of narrowboat owners
becoming prosperous property owners: Iredale in his *Canal Settlement:
Barnton 1775–1845* supplies the instance of John Beech (1759–1840) who
on retirement from his boat bought a house and even extended it. And one

of Worthington and Gilbert's boatmen, an Isaac Jones, bought no fewer than six properties in his dotage when he bid adieu to his life float. These were not folk 'little better than animals' that George Smith portrayed.

We possess a unique glimpse of life on the houseboats of the nineteenth century in the Diary of G.R. Bird, Wharfinger and Carrier of Birmingham, including weather reports and their effect upon canal traffic, 1820–30. Mr Bird is at pains to inform us – rather like another celebrated but fictional diarist of the next century, Mr Pooter – of his regular grand dining habits, which included feasting at the Royal Hotel and entertaining fellow carriers with banquets and fine wines. As a consequence Mr Bird suffered dreadfully with the gout, but he doubtless journeyed to such a state of medical difficulty on a raft of pleasure.

So the moralists' portrayal of narrowboaters leading lives of deprivation and immorality must be taken with a pinch of salt. Admittedly for a hired hand or even a master boatman during a time of depression such as the 1870s, income from a life afloat was precarious, but on the whole a floating life, on rivers or canals, was an occupation of choice for many thousands of adventurous Victorians. So too the incidents of crime on the waterways was not out of proportion. Certainly there was an amount of pilfering and misdemeanour, evinced by the fact that as early as 1802 the principal carriers were constrained to form an Association for the Apprehending and Prosecuting Felons on the waterways. But local magistrate Francis Twemlow reported to the Committee of 1841:

> I have been Chairman of the Staffordshire Quarter Sessions Six Years ... and during that Time I do not think I have had for Trial more than that number of Offences against Boatmen for robbing their cargoes.

Twemlow goes on to state that he knew of 'no cases of Murder but the one I mentioned before, nor any of aggravated assaults'.

The essential honesty of the canal boater hinged on the simple equation of if he did not deliver his cargo, he would be out of a job. While criminality of course existed, it was more particularly concentrated in the canal-side communities that grew up in urban areas. A Constabulary Force Report of 1839 stated that: 'wherever men have been discharged from their regular employment, they have gone to those places where these bodies congregate together, and lived there for months and months, with no ostensible means of livelihood. They infest the banks of our canals to a very great extent.' The dangers came, then, more from these outlying interlopers. A witness for the same Constabulary Report goes on to confess: 'While we engaged upon a course of crime there was no hindrance. We never feared anything for there are no constables on the canals.'

As houseboat dwelling passed into the last few decades of the nineteenth century, the overall theme of the life of this 'society within a society' was that whilst living conditions improved slightly, the work lessened as road haulage increased, until the invention of the combustion engine in the 1880s spelt if not the end then the beginning of the inexorable decline of the canals in the twentieth century. The results of George Smith's pioneering work – the Canal Boat Acts of 1877 and 1884 – were an ambitious attempt to subject the floating community to the same official standards as those living ashore, but historians conclude that the practical effects were mixed. Broadbridge, in his *Living Conditions on Midland Canal Boats* (Transport History, vol. iii, 1970), asserted that:

> while cleanliness improved, overcrowding did not. The standards enforced were clearly low, yet they were constantly being infringed, each year showing twenty or thirty cases of overcrowding or inadequate separation of the sexes.

By 1901 it was estimated that more than 10,000 families were living on board canal boats. Boat dwellers viewed the regular inspections that formed the bulk of the Act's stipulations with increasing distrust and hostility: in 1899, the newly appointed Chief Inspector of Canal Boats reported that: 'the master of a pair of boats complained to me one evening at Salford that the inspector there was the sixth who wanted to see his papers that day.'

Whilst the governmental interventions invited suspicion, it seems that private charities were viewed in a more favourable light. One of the major forces for improvement in the life of boat dwellers in the second half of the nineteenth century was the Boatmen's Friend Society, a typical mid-Victorian philanthropic organisation that began life as the Seamen's Society in 1846 and amalgamated with the Inland Navigation Society in 1851. By all accounts the society achieved much in the provision of welfare and a guidance towards sobriety – certainly by 1910 an old boatman was singing its praises in an edition of *The Waterman* journal of that year:

> Well, governor, I must say the likes of you have helped us chaps a good deal. I've been a boatman for over fifty years, so I can speak like what I know, and that is, that the boat people are a better lot of people than they were, and the likes of you men have done it.

With its mission rooms, kitchens, wash houses, and even entertainments, the Institutes of the Boatmen's Friend Society that dotted the canal-side towns supplied thousands of liveaboards with sanitary assistance, spiritual welfare (what today might be called 'well-being'), and alternatives to the music hall or the public house. They also provided a letter-writing service to the largely illiterate houseboaters, its Birmingham branch writing fifty-four letters for its members in 1908. The missionaries of the Boatmen's Friend Society were by all accounts held in high regard by the boating community, as evinced by this observation by a Special Commissioner in the *Daily Mail* of 1875:

The Canal Boatmen's Mission Hall, Brentford, later renamed the Boatmen's Institute, opened in 1896, with the aim of 'improving the life of water-dwellers'. (Brentford Historical Society)

Bluff, hearty and even jovial in their intercourse with the men and women in the floating homes ... I could see with great pleasure how it was they were looked upon as great friends of the boatman and his little ones.

It is fair to say that by the end of the century, whilst bargees and their families were still viewed with suspicion by some, their reputation had improved. To a great extent they had been enveloped by the embrace of officialdom as their land-based counterparts had been, subject to the same supervision, inspection and overlordship as any other workforce in industrialised Britain. The difference was that the waterways trader, once he had embarked on his voyage, was free to a greater extent than the factory worker, more his own man – especially if he was a 'Number One', a boat owner – subject only to the need for his cargo to be delivered on time. And despite the rise in competition from the railway, life had generally become better by 1900. As the canal-boat inspector of Heston and Isleworth noted in 1891, 'The Acts are in my opinion certainly working well for the lifting up of the people occupying canal boats, and cleanliness and the preventing of overcrowding are the great means.' Perhaps sounder testimony comes from the mouths of the boatmen themselves; interviewed in 1921, aged narrowboat dweller William Bagnall looked back across his long life on the waterways and declared that life on the canals had:

improved in everything to what it was when I was a boy ... the boats are more clean and decent ... Everything has improved.

(Committee on 'Living-in', 1921).

Whilst it was a life of some hardship, a balanced conclusion is that George Smith's portrayal of houseboat dwelling in the nineteenth century as being one of deprivation, squalor and misery is an exaggeration born out of the prejudices of the age towards a community existing outside the mainstream. Certainly the writer Temple Thurston, who lived and worked with them, described boatmen in 1911 as 'Nature's gentlemen'. As ever with these historical judgements, things are not black and white. As the century ended, new challenges lay ahead for the professional boat dweller. Battered by the railways, fresh threats loomed with road improvements and the coming of another monster of Britain's industrial revolution: the internal combustion engine.

Throughout this time the river merchant of course was steadily plying his way along the natural waterways of this island, the growth of his trade powered by the extraordinary expansion of London's docks. London had from the earliest times been the hub of international and internal trade, but in medieval times the goods had largely been transferred midstream from ship to lighterman's barge and vice-versa. There'd been the deep-water harbours of Billingsgate and Queenhithe, of course, and Pepys in the 1660s noted a wet dock in Blackwall holding 'a brave new merchant-man which is to be launched shortly'. But in 1789 the first big purpose-built dock was constructed, the Brunswick, with its vast mast house towering 120ft into the air conveying to all who saw it England's growing maritime power.

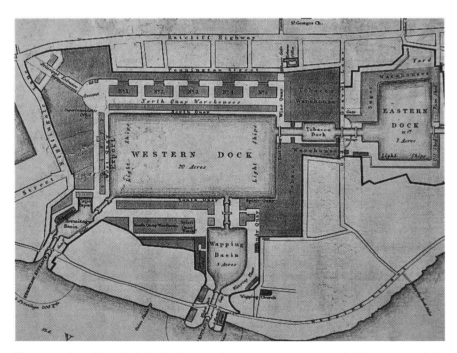

The expansion of London's docks in the early nineteenth century fuelled the growth of the boating population: as early as 1831 Wapping was becoming the hub of world trade and by 1800 12,000 boatmen were living and working on the Thames. (Henry Palmer)

The heyday of the British Empire was approaching, and the life of the riverman entered a new phase.

In part the growth of London's docks was triggered by sheer congestion. By 1800 it is calculated that there were 1,775 vessels suitable only for 545 ships, and in addition, 3,500 barges were moored either waiting to despatch their goods or load up to journey upriver. It was the West India Company Act of 1800 that changed everything, and it was the result, largely, of a united complaint on the parts of the boat owners and ship owners. There were cases of bargemen having to wait days, or even a week, to find a vacant berth to unload. Such a bottleneck was not sustainable, and the result was to transform London's landscape for generations; one might say right up to the 1980s when, after 1,000 years of hegemony, London surrendered its crown as focal point for large cargoes and Docklands became purely a residential and financial centre.

The new docks came thick and fast: there was the 'Upper Pool' stretching from London Bridge to Tower Bridge, and the 'Lower Pool' the other way to Bermondsey. The West India Dock, East India Dock, Blackwall and Surrey Docks, the Regent's Canal Dock and St Katharine's Dock, in 1828, all grew up in the place of the narrow and often fetid streets of medieval London. The Fleet River was closed over and barges no longer had to cramp themselves tightly in the Dowgate. The Thames had always been, as the antiquarian Camden described it, a 'forest of masts', but now it became a broad glistening vista with non-stop two-way traffic. To accommodate the boom, a new highway was built, thrusting its way north-east and aptly named Commercial Road. More docks followed – Victoria, Millwall, Tilbury, Lady Dock, Lavender Pond – and later in the century further deep-water basins for steamships. Many of these docks were invisible from the Thames, hidden behind vast warehouses, around which the rivermen and bargemen flocked to garner their cargoes to take upriver and thence to the heartlands of Britain.

All this growth had a huge impact on the life of the riverboat dweller. With the canals in ascendance, the bargemen operating solely on the rivers declined but did not disappear. The number of watermen – that is to say, bargemen and lightermen working on the Thames – had risen from 3,000 at the end of the sixteenth century to 12,000 by 1800. As the railways became prominent, and then road transport, many boatmen combined canal work with river freight. Rubber, coffee, rum, indigo, pepper, tobacco, tea, dates, canned meat, all spread across the nation on a vast network of boats. And exports were no less fulsome: a single cold store in the Royal Albert Dock could accommodate 250,000 of mutton, the Surrey Docks a million tons of timber, and the West India Dock a million tons of wine.

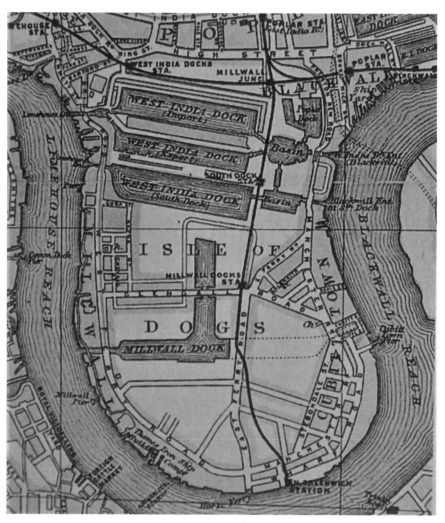

The huge expansion of the London docks meant that by 1899 the Isle of Dogs was like a city within the city.

And what of boating for pleasure? Throughout the period 1750–1900 there had always been leisure boating. Recreational angling aboard a skiff, if not undertaken as a daily ritual of survival, was a form of simply 'messing about on the river', but in the last quarter of the nineteenth century the practice of taking to the waterways in the pursuit of repose expanded exponentially. From the advent of mid-Victorian prosperity when a huge lower-middle and middle class was spawned, vast swathes of the population appeared able to afford a bizarre thing called 'holidaymaking' hitherto the provenance only of the wealthy.

As early as 1555 an enterprising fellow in Oxfordshire had organised a 'pleasure trip' along the Thames from Abingdon to Oxford to witness the executions of Bishops Latimer and Ridley. In the seventeenth century on every Trinity Monday women and girls used to row downriver to Rotherhithe where a great party was held on the river, with much firing of cannon and blowing of trumpets, to celebrate the rivermen who in all weathers steered the nation's cargoes hundreds of miles. These were isolated occasions of course, and day trips, but by the middle of the nineteenth century it was recognised in Parliament that rivers had become more than mere conduits. In the Thames Preservation Act of 1855 it was declared that the river 'has largely come to be used as a place of public recreation and resort; and it is expedient that provision should be made that it should be preserved'. This is a strong indication that waterways were beginning to be recognised *economically* as being not just trade routes but loci of an emerging tourist industry, and it is but a series of short steps from day trips on the water to longer periods of holidaymaking to living permanently afloat. Cheap railway travel in the 1870s and 1880s fuelled this leisure boom, until by 1888 an astonishing 6,768 people were travelling from London to Henley for the famous regatta.

Rivers as places of festivals, pageants and days of leisure were obviously descended from ancient rituals of appeasing the gods of the waterways; and these led in the nineteenth century to the proliferation of a certain type of fashionable houseboat, in which people would congregate for days, weekends, or longer, to view the spectacles. The *Thames Tide & Fashionable River Gazette* of 25 June 1892 (the very existence of such a journal proving the ubiquity of the waterways as new-found places of leisure) was even making recommendations for the decor of houseboats, stipulating very specifically that there should be three rows of plants and lots of hanging baskets. Fetes, fairs and pageants festooned Britain's waterways in the nineteenth century, all of them offering enticing glimpses of rivers as sources of fun and escape from the norms of society. There was a fashion in the latter part of the century for 'illuminated' boats – vessels set on fire that drifted down the rivers to the accompaniment of brass bands. At Bourne End a large houseboat was disguised as the Man in the Moon.

These river festivals led to the acquiring of a certain 'reputation' amongst riverside towns for licentiousness: they became refuges from the overweening morality of the day, places where people felt freer to indulge their appetites. Maidenhead, for example, acquired the nickname 'the hymen of London'.

Another facet of river life that fed into the gradual growth of 'houseboat living' was the phenomenon of 'restaurant boats' that were in themselves extensions of the pleasure gardens that were all the rage in cities and large towns, particularly London, in the late-seventeenth and eighteenth centuries. It is no accident, I believe, that houseboat communities that grew up in the twentieth century were often located near these pleasure gardens of old, such as the still-flourishing floating village of Chelsea Reach, Cheyne Walk, in London, which clusters around the former Cremorne Gardens. One of the later gardens, Cremorne opened in the 1840s, occupying many acres of Thames bankside. Theatres, banqueting saloons, dance halls: with amenities such as these, it is no surprise that Victorians would make a week of it, and congregate in 'houseboats' along the shore.

As early as 1636 one John Rookes applied to open a floating restaurant on the Thames, with the aim of it serving 'such provisions and necessaries as are vendible in the Tavernes and Victuallinge houses especially in the summer season'. It was but a short hop from water-borne restaurants to floating hotels, the most famous of these being The Folly, a haunt of Samuel Pepys that was launched in the 1660s and lay midstream at some point near where Cleopatra's Needle is now located. A vast houseboat with numerous floors, bars, promenades and overnight rooms, it became famous for vice, being described as 'a musical summer house for the entertainment of quality where they might meet and ogle one another', and was immortalised in song in 1719, when Tom D'Urfey wrote his 'A Touch of the Thames':

When Drapers smugg'd Prentices
With exchange girls mostly jolly,
After shop was shut up
Could sail to the folly.

In the nineteenth century a genre of 'river literature' sprang up, pioneered by writers like Robert Louis Stevenson, whose *An Inland Voyage* of 1878 chronicled his journey by single-sailed kayak through the canals of Belgium and France. It was the beginning of a craze, and it was not long before 'holidaying' on the waterways morphed into permanent living. On his journey Stevenson came across many 'gypsy-like' families living aboard their barges, and – understandably for the 26-year-old romantic budding writer – he painted a picturesque portrait of the lifestyle:

> There should be many contented spirits on board, for such a life is both to travel and to stay at home ... and for the bargee, in his floating home, 'travelling abed,' it is merely as if he were listening to another man's story or turning the leaves of a picture book in which he had no concern.

From that time the world of river and canal life was sundered in twain, creating a permanent division between the waterways as work and leisure. For the bargee plying his trade between the grim Gas Basin of Birmingham down to the soot-caked caverns of London, living afloat was largely drudgery and duty, but there now emerged a new class, those who *chose* to live on board a vessel as a means of escape from industrial civilisation.

Nowhere is this stark contrast more vividly expressed than in *The Flower of Gloster*, an account written in 1911 by E. Temple Thurston of a canal journey from the Midlands to London. Thurston complains:

> You only have to go into the Black Country to know what can be done with a wonderful world when God delivers it into the hands of man ... The stream of molten metal flows through the veins and arteries of a great nation ... but what a price to pay, and what a coinage to pay it in ... those belching furnaces and that poisoned land must make you marvel as you pass by.

Thurston's was clearly a philosophic perception born from an artistic rejection of industrial civilisation and a romanticising of canal life as somehow 'prelapsarian', though of course it was nothing of the kind – indeed, canals were at the forefront of the industrial revolution that had so transformed the British landscape. Whilst eulogising the rustic scenery of Warwickshire, once he had reached open country, Thurston's soul stiffens and he condemns the urban Midlands and its 'charred heart' as 'an awful yet wonderful part of the world'.

This was a boat dweller in search of something from the aquatic life that the working bargee or river trader would if not reject completely then treat with diffidence: for them the waterways were a means of survival, not a thing of leisure or frivolous aesthetic nourishment. That's not to say the average boatmen and his family were blind to the beauties of landscape, but more important was a sense of independence, a liberation from the thrall of factory and mill and workshop.

The late nineteenth century saw the flourishing of artistic and literary movements at odds with industrial civilisation: the Arts and Crafts movement, harking back to the localised medieval ethos of cottage industry and Guild; and the Aesthetic vortices of the Pre-Raphaelites and post-Romantics of the 1890s. The notion of houseboat living as a refuge was born in this era, fed by the ennui of a middle-class and upper-middle-class intelligentsia seeing their country scarred by the relentless advance of railway, factory and 'Satanic mills'. Amidst this encroachment of mechanisation, a lust for rustic liberty flowered. Part and parcel with this movement was the model-dwelling phenomena such as Bourneville in Birmingham, housing for workers built in the 'rural village' style – cottages boat livers would presumably eye in envy or disdain as they drifted by on the Grand Junction.

Houseboat living for pleasure was clearly an established phenomenon by 1881 when the artist George Dunlop Leslie published his memoir of living on the Thames, *Our River*. A Victorian painter of light genres – *September Sunshine*, *The Author's Punt*, etc. – Leslie was highly regarded as a post-Pre-Raphaelite (if such a school existed), dividing his time between a comfortable abode in St John's Wood and a cottage in Wallingford. A devotee of the punt, Leslie was a familiar sight ploughing through the water past the meadows and villages of the Upper Thames. He crystallised his love for waterways in his book, and *Our River* became a central work in the canon of aquatic literature.

A passionate follower of river life as a means of exercising one's physical and artistic muscles, Leslie was oddly suspicious of the houseboat dweller:

> They look inviting and snug with their little windows and curtains, their bird cages and pots of flowers, the smoke curling up from the kitchen chimney and the cooking and washing up going on inside; but I cannot help thinking it must be a little tedious.

Houseboats built for pleasure rather than work date back to the seventeenth century, but late Victorian England was the heyday of the pleasure craft, culminating in the magnificent *Astoria*, impresario Fred Karno's three-bedroomed vessel still moored at Hampton.

He added somewhat disdainfully, 'If not employed on some active business, such as cleaning or cooking, the occupants very often wear rather a blasé expression.'

Notwithstanding his derogatory tone, it is clear from Leslie's casual mention of houseboats that they were by the time of writing, the early 1880s, a common sight on Britain's waterways (as distinct from the working barges, which had existed for centuries). He goes on to paint an idyllic picture of river life as an artists' retreat: 'There are generally a good many artists at Hurley, and two or three houseboats can usually be seen moored off the lock-house.' Hurley sits on a particularly picturesque stretch of the Thames that glides between Marlow and Temple, and was plainly a sought-after locale for painters – Samuel Fildes created his famous *Fair Quiet and Sweet Rest* in one of the reedy backwaters near Harleyford Manor.

Many of these houseboats, then, represented a new breed of weekend boat dweller. Despite his faint distrust, Leslie wasn't averse to socialising with them, and he befriended many a neighbour who lived on the water:

> Whilst we were at Marlow, Sir Henry Thompson came up the river in a houseboat, and anchored off Bisham. He was very pleased with this reach, and lived in his boat whenever he could get away from town. He is an accomplished cook, and he and his son contrive most excellent dishes on board the boat. I could often, in the afternoon, when passing, smell a savoury stew going on.

Leslie goes on to describe an unfortunate event that led them to draw upon the local river population for assistance:

> Mr. Alma Tadema came down to see him for a day or two, and they sketched away from the deck of the boat together. One evening, I had been punting Sir Henry about on the river, and on returning to his houseboat, as he was stepping from the punt, he dropped his cigarette-case into the water; it was large and heavy with a good deal of silver mounting on it, and sank to the bottom directly. There was nothing to be done in the dark, but the next morning he procured the assistance of a diver, the son of a fisherman at Marlow, who after one or two failures brought it up out of eight feet of water, to the delight of Sir Henry and Tadema.

098. HENLEY-ON-THAMES. THE REGATTA COURSE. I.

Since 1839 houseboats have gathered at Henley for the world-famous Regatta. For some, it was a short step from holidaying aboard to seeking a permanent life afloat.

A few miles upriver stood Henley, of course, whose Regatta, first established in 1839, was rapidly becoming one of the highlights of the British summer season, and which as a consequence became a magnet for occasional houseboat dwellers far and wide. In a panegyric chapter of his book, Leslie paints a wildly chaotic picture of Regatta-mania: 'Directly the racing boats have passed, the course is rapidly covered again by boats of every description: there are gigs, skiffs, wherries, stout oak sailing-boats, canoes and punts …' And houseboats, for which Leslie, in a *volte-face,* now has nothing but praise:

Jerome K. Jerome's *Three Men in a Boat* of 1889 – perhaps the greatest work of inland waterways literature.

Houseboats are particularly convenient at the Regatta; they accommodate a large party, and afford a sense of security from the rain, which on one of the days is a well-known proverbial certainty. No better can be certain than the roof of a houseboat for seeing the racing from, and with a good lunch below, a pleasant party, and a boat or two to move about in occasionally, in my view the houseboat affords quite the best means of enjoying the day to perfection.

Perhaps the most famous artistic expression of this late-nineteenth-century boating renaissance was Jerome K. Jerome's *Three Men in a Boat* of 1889, a book that catapulted the diffident would-be actor and journalist from Walsall into the front rank of literary humour. In many ways a comic riposte to Dunlop Leslie's more solemn and elegiac tome, Jerome's classic immortalised the adventures of that late-Victorian and Edwardian phenomenon, the *Knut, Dandy,* or *Masher* – in short, the man-about-town who once or twice a year sought to abandon the noise, clamour and pleasures of the city for a week or so, and go and live on the river.

Jerome was of the generation that caught the Thames before the urbanisation of Greater London changed the first 15 miles of its landscape forever: 'There were lovely stretches then between Richmond and Staines, meadows and cornfields,' he wrote in his memoirs of 1926, a paean proving that by the 1920s things had all changed utterly: 'At first, we used to have the river almost to ourselves; but year by year it got more crowded and Maidenhead became our starting-point.' Harris, George and 'J.', of course, did not reside in a houseboat in the strictest definition of the word, but in a covered skiff: 'Sometimes we would fix up a trip of three or four days or a week, doing the thing in style and camping out.' A hobbyist boater, certainly, but ironically Jerome echoed Leslie's occasional distaste for the houseboat, imagining, in the spirit of the book, that he (or at least his character, 'J') was a true 'man of the river', in spiritual alliance with the old bargees and the proper sailors, sceptical of the upstart hobbyists and weekend sailors who took to the water from mere whim and idle fancy.

The newfangled steam launch became the bane of all aquatic purists, and Jerome was no exception. In a marvellous passage in *Three Men in a Boat* – a passage that is as much social history as it is situational comedy – Jerome describes the trio loading up with supplies at Marlow and parading back to their boat near the bridge, followed by dozens of boys laden with goods of all descriptions:

> When we got to the landing-stage, the boatman said, 'Let me see, sir; was yours a steam-launch or a houseboat?' On our informing him it was a double-sculling skiff, he seemed surprised. We had a good deal of trouble with steam-launches that morning. It was just before Henley week, and they were going up in large numbers; some by themselves, some towing houseboats. I do hate steam-launches; I suppose every rowing man does. I never see a steam-launch but I feel I should like to lure it to a lonely part of the river, and there, in the silence and the solitude, strangle it.

After 1880, then, industrial boating and leisure boating maintained an uneasy coexistence. Old lock-keepers would refer to the river dwellers who didn't make a living from the waterways as 'Noddy Boatmen' who 'didn't know where they were going', contrasting them with the professional stalwarts of the water whose gimlet eyes were ever fixed on each current and eddy. But creek by creek, marina by marina, little houseboat communities began to spring up, gradually asserting their right to a place on the waterways as strong as the working boats. And it is to these communities that we now turn, as a new century dawned, with its challenges to the hegemony of the canals, and the emergence of a large yet motley swathe of people choosing to lead their lives upon the water.

4

TWILIGHT
ᘐᕤᘐ OF THE TRADERS ᘐᕤᘐ

1900–1945

As they steered their hulks silently along the placid waterways of Victorian England, the bargees of the golden age of canals could scarcely have dreamt that their vessels – laden with coal, salt, wine, fancy goods – would end up nearly a century later as houseboats for a new generation.

Yet countless numbers of those working barges did. In the houseboat community at Benfleet in Essex, which still exists today, there is a remarkable record of some of the old boats that were used as dwellings before and after the Second World War. Their very age speaks of their former lives as workhorses of the canal network: '*Hearts of Oak*, London, 45 net tons, built 1879. *Henry*, 49 net tons, built 1865; hulked Benfleet Creek. *Invicta*, Rochester, 56 net tons, built 1877, 77ft. *Mary Jane*, Rochester, 42 net tons, 1877. *Sunrise*, Rochester, 50 net tons, built 1889, 80ft. House barge at Benfleet, finally broken up.' And so on. These details from the *Sailing Barge Compendium* published by the Society of Sailing Barge Research are a chronicle of how a vast transport industry metamorphosed into floating yet often sedentary communities.

In the span of sixty years, from 1900 to 1960, industrial carriage on Britain's canal network all but ceased, and the fact that these noble working barges listed above ended their days as houseboats is a clear snapshot of the fate of water transport in the twentieth century – a destiny that can be characterised as stubborn persistence in the face of inexorable decline. A major change was the decline of the 'Number Ones', those families owning their own boats. Increasingly unable to compete with the rise of cheaper road haulage, many of these owner-boatmen had no choice but to sell their vessels to the big carrying companies and continue as employees, or give up the business completely, resulting in the barges above ending as houseboats.

One big revolution in the working boats of the early twentieth century was, of course, the onset of steam. The huge side paddles of the major river steamers of the USA were naturally wholly impractical for Britain's narrow canals, but a small yet hugely influential invention by Francis Pettit Smith, the screw propellor, meant that steam power could gradually find its way onto England's waterways. Progress was slow, despite the first steam narrowboats appearing as early as 1860 for the carrying company Fellows, Morton & Clayton on the Grand Junction, the locks of the Grand Junction being wide enough to hold two vessels side by side so the steam barge could haul its butty alongside. But gradually the waterways of England, and large numbers of boat dwellers, transferred to these newfangled steam barges and 'Puffers'.

Benfleet Creek, where nineteenth-century working barges became twentieth-century houseboats.

The success of the steam barge lay, of course, in its never tiring; unlike the traditional horse, many were used in the 'fly' trade, i.e. working non-stop, day and night. Five men usually lived on the 'steamer' and three on the butty. The voyages of these steam barges were fast, and they were soon outrunning their more sedate horse-drawn companions: a journey from Limehouse Basin in London, at the end of the Regent's Canal, to Fazeley in Birmingham, took a mere forty-four hours, a voyage of 151 miles and 161 locks.

One huge advantage bestowed by steam on the canals was the use of tugs to haul barges through the long tunnels with no towpaths, rendering the ancient practice of 'legging' unnecessary. Much as this would have led to the chagrin of many permanent leggers, at Blisworth Tunnel near Stoke Bruerne, Northamptonshire on the Grand Union Canal – a daunting 1¾ miles long – tugs to tow the barges were a godsend.

With the rise of steam came also a new type of houseboat: the Puffer, or more accurately the Clyde Puffer, given its birthplace on the Forth & Clyde Canal. While still recognisably a canal barge and a descendant of the ancient Western barge of medieval times, with a flat bottom and rounded stern, the Puffer had a distinctive vertical funnel, with a cabin aft for the captain and accommodation for the crew in the fo'c'sle up in the bows. Puffers soon became a familiar sight on the waterways of Scotland, and it wasn't long before their versatility allowed them to venture forth to become coastal traders, and to the islands of the west coast.

It was steam put to another use, of course, that was one cause of the slow decline in canal transport, but more important than the railway steam engine, it was the rise to eminence of the internal combustion engine and the proliferation of road haulage that did it for the waterways. It didn't happen overnight: it was a long journey for barges, such as the *Hearts of Oak* or *Mary Jane* between 1900 and their sedate yet lowly end on the mudflats of Essex, and it is a journey that began as a heyday. After all, a huge new canal was being built as late as 1894 in the form of the mighty Manchester Ship Canal. Designed for boats and ships up to 50,000 tons to carry cargo from Merseyside deep into the heart of Manchester, it could not rival Panama or Suez but certainly gave those gigantic cousins a run for their money. With its huge locks – the biggest being 600ft by 60ft – the humble bargee was often dwarfed by its scale. It was the last great achievement of the Canal Age, and like its predecessors was built in the traditional way, with armies of navvies to shift the estimated 76 million tons of soil. Living in shanty towns on its banks, these roistering, singing, hard-drinking sons of the soil were the descendants of James Brindley's first legions of migrant workers all those years ago in 1761 when the Bridgewater Canal was built. But one cannot help but look on the Manchester Ship Canal as a poignant – yet noble and fitting – swansong to the age of man-made waterways for trade purposes. Another golden age lay ahead of course – that of canals as places of life and leisure after 1945 – but that story lies ahead.

At the beginning of the century the boater's life was still benefitting from Victorian prosperity, and an improvement in conditions as overseen by the inspections and stipulations of the Canal Acts effected by George Smith. Yet as the decades passed, both the practical living arrangements and the economic life of the bargee and his family became squeezed.

The Canal Acts had laid down the minimum living space on board working barges, for with single horse-drawn boats life could be crowded, but the coming of the motor-driven houseboat presented its own problems. A feature of the early diesel boats was a disproportionately large engine room, which compromised living space. More and more often, families would operate two boats, the barge and the butty, the latter being a smaller vessel used for a mixture of accommodation and light goods that was not power driven, and the main barge for heavy goods that pulled the butty behind.

Financially, the income of a bargee and his family never again saw the heights it reached during the most prosperous years of the nineteenth century. Boatmen were paid by the tonnage, and as the condition of the canals deteriorated, were forced to carry lighter and lighter cargoes. Only as late as 1940 was a minimum wage for a barge captain laid down by statute: £5 a week, the equivalent of £328 at 2021 rates.

The first half of the twentieth century saw an inexorable encroachment of 'officialdom' upon the lives of those who lived and worked afloat, an attempt to wrest canal living into the modern age through regulation, until the 1950s when the entire industry was nationalised and came under the sway of the petty official, the regulator and the civil servant. This 'modernisation' of the working boatman's life was fiercely resisted, and there grew a counterculture of defending the liveaboard's life, independence and self-reliance, with writers like G.K. Chesterton and Hilaire Belloc, whose tirades against modernity were made with broad brushstrokes but which included calls for the protection of the bargee's way of life. The familiar calls for 'boat people' to be more educated were made, and indeed literacy was a problem. At home on the waterways, the boating family was largely lost in a sea of meaningless symbols when setting foot on land. As late as 1950 the canal writer L.T.C. Rolt was declaring that illiteracy amongst the floating population was something felt by them keenly, and was motivating many to leave the migrant life and move ashore.

The Blisworth Tunnel, Northamptonshire. When steam tugs began towing boats through in the late nineteenth century, many houseboaters celebrated the end of having to 'leg' their vessels the arduous 3,076 yd.

Another pressure on the old way of life was the rise in 'day boating', i.e. canals divided into sections whereby a bargee would carry a load from one section to another, with his wife and family living ashore. This had actually been the practice for many years on the Staffordshire & Worcestershire Canal, but it never really took off to a significant extent on other waterways – if it had, it would of course have spelt the end of the family boat. Day boating was looked down on by the long-distance boater – it acquired the derogatory nickname 'joey boating'. For the ancient bargee family a 'joey boater' had no pride in his vessel, merely treating it as a workhorse: it was by very definition in fact no longer a home or even a houseboat. Many boatmen found it anathema to take over anyone else's boat for the day – it simply ran counter to everything in his being, and the notion that these were simply vehicles for cargo was outrageous. Did they not possess the same anthropomorphic resonance as ships at sea, with the same feminine pronouns, 'she' and 'her'? For the ancient houseboat dweller the vessel was a living, breathing member of the family.

Painting a picture of life on Britain's rivers and canals from 1900 to 1945 draws on many sources, but a surprisingly vivid portrait can be found in fiction. A.P. Herbert's novel *The Water Gipsies*, published in 1930, is so rich and detailed that it reaches back through the decades, etching a vivid portrait of family life on the waterways that hadn't changed for more than half a century. It has rightly become a keynote text in the genre of houseboat fiction.

One of the most famous 'houseboaters' of the interwar years, A.P. Herbert (1890–1971) was a barrister, MP, writer and humourist, and in his life achieved many things, one of the most notable of which was to become the most famous houseboat dweller of his age. He brought his family up on a large hulking barge moored up at Hammersmith, and would often cruise downstream to his job at the Houses of Parliament. Indeed, when the very first air-raid siren sounded across London in 1939, his houseboat, the *Water Gypsy*, was anchored off Speaker's Steps by Westminster Bridge, and was cheered off and saluted by MPs as he sailed off upstream to begin his war work. His role as a driving force in the River Emergency Service in the Second World War will be explored later in the chapter, but a combination of his naval service in the Great War and his love of the Thames led him to become one of the greatest champions of living afloat in the twentieth century. A Pathé News broadcast of 1946 paid him the following glowing tribute: 'No one has done so much to plead for the neglected water highways of Britain as the famous wit, author, playwright, Member of Parliament and ex-Petty Officer in His Majesty's Navy.'

The importance of an MP and a leading barrister choosing to live afloat cannot be overestimated as a signal to the rest of society that this was not merely an eccentric, whimsical act: it was something rooted deep in the DNA of the British character – and his influence undoubtedly led to many adopting the aquatic way of life.

Herbert poured his intimate knowledge of life as a houseboater on the Thames and 'up the Cut' into his 1930 novel *The Water Gipsies*: indeed, so crammed is it with first-hand knowledge of living and working on the waterways that it transcends fiction and becomes a unique historical document. Passages refer to 'those who dwell on the river at Hammersmith', proving that pockets of houseboating communities were blossoming along the Thames just as boating communities clustered at hubs along the canal system, like Stoke Bruerne or Braunston. The first houseboat 'villages' on rivers were, at first, people who also worked the canals, like the protagonists, the Green family, who work the Grand Union (formerly the Junction) but also itinerant families like the Bells. Mr Bell is a musician, a rather unsuccessful one, whose work in a London orchestra dries up and who has a propensity for the betting shop. His indigence – and widowerhood – leads him to live with his two daughters on a ramshackle barge moored beside a jetty in old Hammersmith. At telling moments, when people learn of the Bells being houseboaters, they invariably respond with 'what a fantastic place to live!, how too romantic!' – to which Jane replies 'ugh, too damp!' To the land dwellers, then, already by the 1920s, to live on the water was beginning to be perceived as bohemian and 'madly gay' – a far cry from the thinly veiled scorn and distaste which previous generations of liveaboards were subject to. We are glimpsing the beginnings of the perception of living afloat as a way of life distinct from *working on the water*.

Even in the late 1920s illiteracy was evidently still a problem for the working boat dweller: in *The Water Gipsies*, Fred Green the canal boatman can neither read nor write, explaining that the lock-keepers take dictation then read out the boater's letters to the recipient when they arrive at the same lock. This ancient practice was still continuing into the interwar period and beyond (L.T.C. Rolt writing in 1950 noted that illiteracy was such a problem that the canal worker was 'lost' when stepping ashore).

Sir A.P. Herbert, author, barrister and MP, the most famous houseboater of his age.

The landscape and way of life of the twentieth-century houseboater is laid out in a broad canvas in the pages of *The Water Gipsies*: from the descriptions of the boat dwellers going 'wooding' in their row boats on the tidal Thames for fuel – catching up floating planks and other flotsam – to the deep swathes of countryside beyond old Rickmansworth up to Stoke Bruerne and the Blisworth Tunnel, where dozens of boats would tie up in the evening and wait for the tug in the morning to haul them through the 1¾-mile-long cavern. Jane 'the half-boater' joins the old Green family, who've lived aboard for generations, on a voyage into the heart of aquatic England.

It is a journey that starts on the Thames at Hammersmith, with the barge *Prudence* first wending its way to the mouth of the ancient River Brent, opposite Kew Gardens. The river mouth here was a settlement since pre-Roman days: indeed, there is a letter extant from AD 705 detailing a meeting of West Saxon tribes and East Saxon tribes at the village near the bourne – the place where the Brent met the Thames. Roman goods and artifacts have been found deep in the mud here, indicating Brentford was used for river trading from the earliest times. And so it continued: here in 1855 was built the great Brentford Dock, a major hub of transfer between barges and the Great Western Railway. The warehouses and wharves at Brentford have gone now, though by the mouth of the Grand Union Canal there are still extensive boatyards.

It's no coincidence that these great trading hubs on rivers and canals became, many decades later, the home of houseboat communities now unconnected with the movement of goods. Waterman's Park, Chiswick, and all along the river at Brentford, many houseboats are moored, though in recent times a shadow has hung over them, their stability threatened by the legal tussles over much unregistered stretches of the riverbank. This battle will be explored in a later chapter.

The River Brent steers north for 3 miles as part of the tidal Thames, then joins the Grand Union (formerly the Grand Junction) that takes the boatman west to Hayes then north to Denham and the Midlands. In 1930 Brentford Lock was thick with the shouts of warehousemen and bargees loading up with flour and grain from the breadbasket of the southern counties for the cities of the north. *The Water Gipsies* is a snapshot of an

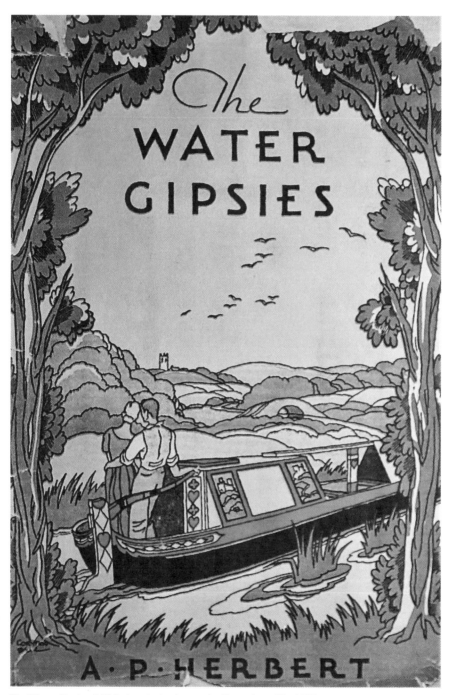

The Water Gipsies, A.P. Herbert's classic novel of houseboat life, 1930.

England long gone, with Ealing described as a 'rustic solitude'. The heroine Jane, though she lives on a houseboat with her sister and musician father, now feels as though she is in a 'strange land', among this ancient, almost foreign race of bargees, or 'boatmen' as the Green family insist on calling themselves.

It is the women of the boats she feels most afeared of, with their dark eyes, heavy shawls and suspicious glances; the men, while intrigued, greet her with cheery cries. Babies crawl about the roofs of the boats, smoke puffs up from the little chimneys.

The journey in *The Water Gipsies* is of the traditional two boats, *Adventure* and *Prudence*, hauled by the horse Beauty, sometimes towed alongside each other, at other times in single file, according to the traffic. The cabins are festooned with brass knobs and decorated with the classic hearts, roses and castles motifs – roses for beauty, hearts for romance, castles for worldly honour, or perhaps an ancient dream of fortitude and permanence. After all, the most transient home is a boat, the most permanent a castle: the two edifices could not stand in greater contrast.

Mrs Green is as traditional as her boat: her head shawled, feet clad in boots of black leather like her husband's, hair bound tightly into thin plaits. From her ears dangle green glass earrings and on her breast hangs a brooch containing a photograph of her husband. In the cabin are vases full of wild flowers plucked from the hedgerows by Mr Green as he plods along with the horse.

The ascent of the River Brent for 3 miles until it meets the Grand Union was, and is, a hard slog: at Hanwell there are no fewer than seven locks in a mere quarter of a mile. With 150 locks between Brentford and Birmingham, the rigour of the working life afloat soon hits home to the novel's heroine, Jane Bell, who is deciding whether to embrace the liveaboard life and marry her beau, Fred Green. The importance of the lock to the boatman and his family is hammered home. Here the bargees draw their water, buy their bread and milk; the gates are opened, some with a windlass, some with a beam; contact is made between families passing each other, not to be seen again for a week or more; and behind the lock is often an old inn sitting on the banks of a tributary or cutaway, where some boating families stable their horses and tie up for the night.

For A.P. Herbert, a barrister writing in the 1920s, the locks of the Grand Union seemed 'endless', but the ritual of passing through had a profound effect on his imaginative sensibilities: the music of the water, whether a slow trickle or a full cascade over the pound, the hooting of the owls, the lovers leaning over the high gates on summer evenings. At Hanwell there is a touch of gothic to the romance of the canal journey, for the waterway rises up the hill past the famous lunatic asylum, in a series of dramatic terraces.

On the Grand Union proper now, the River Brent meanders off to distant Barnet while the man-made waterway plunges west to Southall and West Drayton, which in 1930 was a grim forest of factories, warehouses and rows of 'mean houses'. Then the open fields of Cowley and the oak-dotted meadows of Kings Langley and Rickmansworth, where the railway and the road is lost. The boats slide beneath the cavernous canopies of huge trees. For Herbert this is where canal life plunged back in time, where it was hard for him to conceive that this was the same man-made waterway that passes between the tall factories and warehouses of Paddington and Limehouse. The only signs of civilisation on this stretch of the Grand Union are the odd cottage garden suddenly blazing with flowers. He had reached a certain wilderness.

As the Grand Union reaches the Chilterns once again the locks come thick and fast, and boatmen would often not wait till they came upon them but strode ahead of their horses, opening the lock gates in preparation. So busy was this reach of the Cut that many locks were, as the boat people were wont to say, 'against them' – that is, the pound was occupied by vessels travelling in the opposite direction. To reach an empty lock was a luxury.

Even as late as 1930, when A.P. Herbert was writing *The Water Gipsies,* the tradition of only marrying a husband or wife 'from the Cut' persisted; indeed, it is one of the dominant themes of the book. The hero, Fred Green, is engaged to Jane Bell who is only a 'half-boatwoman' because she lives on a non-working barge; he receives a letter from another canal girl, Ruth:

Dear Fred, we are loading timber at Marley's for Braunston Saturday night with luck hoping I may see you Fred.

Courtship on the water is a difficult, haphazard affair, fraught with rare opportunities for meeting, narrow chances missed. In this sense the lore and practice of boat life matched that of the Romanies, who also tended to wed within their community. Why? It was very probably the singularity, the uniqueness of the liveaboard life that was the driving force behind the custom. 'If you weren't attuned to the life, how could you cope?' In *The Water Gipsies* it is referred to as a 'calling' – indeed Jane Bell describes the 'call of the water' as an almost spiritual dynamic that fuels her decision in the end to marry Fred Green and lead a life afloat, and her acceptance by the boat-dwelling community. Herbert, through his protagonist Jane, pays homage to the spiritual power of living aboard a barge:

> Their motion was as gentle as the coming of sleep; their blunt, round prows did not divide the water, but caress it; there was no sound but the ripple along the shore and the slow clip-clop of Beauty's feet, and these said 'Peace', and brought peace to Jane's soul.

Despite these epiphanic moments, Jane's decision to settle on the water permanently is not one easily reached. A vivid picture of the 1¾-mile-long Blisworth Tunnel near Stoke Bruerne is a dramatic episode in Herbert's book, and hammers home the extraordinary slog boat people had to endure on a daily and weekly basis. Even when no 'legging' was required after the proliferation of the tug-boat, which would haul a caravan of barges through the endless underground passageways. The experience was not one for the faint-hearted, and took its toll on the psyche. The passage is clearly based on personal experience: Herbert describes the clammy walls of the suffocating cavern, the darkness alleviated only by lonely rays of light signifying occasional air holes, the echo of the boats bumping against the sides and the only visible thing in the impenetrable darkness being the faint lantern swinging on the tug's stern far ahead, but only then when the long line of boats would be turning a long curved corner. With a row of boats continuously ploughing through, the Blisworth Tunnel was constantly full of sulphurous fumes; the vast weight of the hill could be sensed above the boatmen's heads; and as perhaps the ultimate demonstration that the whole experience was a kind of inferno, the black water beneath them was alive with thousands of squirming, swimming rats.

In the 1920s people living on the canals as a life choice as distinct from work were still few and far between. In Herbert's book the trading barges only come across one: 'a long house-boat, one of the rare pleasure-vessels seen on the canal, was lying above through which she had just passed.' But as the decades passed and canal trade declined, it is clear that the main hubs of commerce on the waterways – both rivers and canals – metamorphosed into residential communities. Yet even as late as 1950 L.T.C Rolt noted in his *The Inland Waterways of England* that, with the exception of the Norfolk Broads and the Thames, hardly anyone was actually cruising the waterways for pleasure, a phenomenon that was to dramatically change, of course, partly as a direct result of Rolt's work in forming the Inland Waterway's Association and spearheading the reconstruction and renovation of many of Britain's canals. At the time of *The*

To the relief of many, the advent of the tug boat meant the end of the tortuous art of 'legging' through the canal network's tunnels.

Water Gipsies, 1930, there was still trade enough, but there is a prescient glimpse of the nature of houseboating that was to come when Brentford – the main locale of the bargee element of the story – is on Bank Holiday, and all the painted boats tie up for the weekend. Herbert describes the scene of dozens of idle boats tethered alongside each other up and down river and in the great Brentford dock itself as a 'floating camp', which it became on a permanent basis, of course, after the war.

Woodbridge in Suffolk is another locale that similarly metamorphosed from trade to permanent houseboat occupation. From Anglo-Saxon times the town had been known for its shipbuilding, a thriving industry that shifted to yacht-building in the nineteenth and twentieth centuries. Ideally situated a few miles inland on the broad River Deben, its tide mills still stand today, and when its marina was built in 1963 it was the largest in Britain. Whisstock's Boat Builders began in 1926, on a patch of drained marshland, and from that date to 1939 Claude Whisstock built an extraordinary 127 boats, mainly the Deben Four-Tonner, a compact yet sturdy residential yacht that with its double cabin and single sail has rightly become a classic. During the Second World War, Whisstock even managed to up production for the war effort, building an incredible 200 boats – trawlers, lifeboats, etc. – after the war returning to leisure vessels. With its large and protected waters, this inland reach of the Deben was an ideal site for a 'houseboat village' to become established, and the day and weekend boaters gradually became a permanent, settled community.

The most striking economic change in Britain as far as transportation of goods is concerned in this period was the growth of road haulage, an expansion that came at the expense of both the railways and the canals. While almost all categories of rail freight declined between the wars, the number of goods vehicles on the roads increased five times to 488,000 by 1939, the great majority owned by small independent operators. This bit deep into the canal way of life. On a human level, this change led L.T.C. Rolt to declare, in his 1939 book *Narrow Boat*, that the old stock of canal folk would soon become an extinct race. Delightful though Rolt's book is, and a classic tome of waterway literature, it is an elegy to a way of life, almost a regretful funeral oration. The author mourns the fact that the traditional boatman and his family is tending to leave the waterways, and is being replaced by people 'off the land', with a reputation for squalid living and a lack of pride. This judgement, of course, is a personal one but is clearly based on Rolt's perception as he set out to journey round the canal system in his boat *Cressy*. He travelled to Banbury on the Grand Union, traversed the Trent, then turned south down the Shropshire Canal, reaching Coventry, then dropping down to the Oxford Canal. His journey, on the eve of the Second World War, paints a portrait of life on the waterways at a crossroads, to employ a non-aquatic metaphor. Behind him lay canal life as a job, an industry, a profession; ahead of him lay the waterways as places of leisure, of an alternative lifestyle. If Herbert was the gentleman poet of houseboat living, Rolt was the tireless campaigner for the continuation of the canals as a working environment, while knowing deep in his heart that those days were numbered.

Whisstock's Boat Builders, Woodbridge, Suffolk. Between 1926 and 1939 Claude Whisstock built 127 small boats, most famously the Deben Four-Tonner, a compact residential yacht. The River Deben is still home to houseboats today.

Rolt regrets the fading away of the narrowboater's garb: no more does he see on the Cut the proud captain wearing trousers of buff corduroy or dark mock-moleskin, waistcoats and coats with high lapels; rare now is the sight of the boatwoman clad in boots laced to the calf, full-pleated skirts and tight-waisted dresses, in cold weather the heavy shawl draped round her strong shoulders and the ubiquitous black bonnet. So scarce in fact are these canal folk of old that Rolt's soul is suddenly uplifted when he comes across a barge containing a family that has stuck to the old ways; on the Warwickshire Canal he suddenly sees a woman at the tiller of a passing boat that could have sprung straight from the nineteenth century, who to the 'wonder and delight' of the author is wearing the classic black bonnet. He pours scorn on the group of land women standing in a huddle in Factory Street near the canal, gossiping in their mass-produced clothes.

Rolt was a romantic, that is clear, but his work is a classic in the waterways canon in that it captures that long, long moment when canals slowly ceased to be industrial arteries of Britain and became, by the 1960s, places only of leisure and lifestyle. En route he marks other changes in the houseboater's life: while still remaining largely illiterate, by 1939 most narrowboaters had wirelesses, and on his voyage Rolt would hear almost every evening the strains of the popular melodies of the day wafting over the slightly misted waters – 'Daisy Bell', 'Two Lovely Black Eyes'. But the wireless was a rare foray by the canal folk into the realms of twentieth-century technology. One very old boatman engages Rolt in conversation about his one and only trip in a 'moty car' and complains that the vehicle went so fast it left him breathless. And in a delightful episode in the book, a young policeman leaning over the parapet of a bridge on the Oxford Canal mocks the slowness of the bargee gliding by beneath. The old bargee, without pausing, fires back that if everyone went as slow as he there wouldn't be any trouble in the world, adding – as the boat disappeared beneath the stone bridge – that if that were the case then the policeman would in all probability be out of a job.

The old boat builders, while being affected by the rise of road haulage, still persisted between the wars, though their work constructing trading barges shifted gradually into maintenance and repair. Rolt has his boat *Cressy* fitted out by Tooley's of Banbury, an old firm stretching back to the nineteenth century. The design of *Cressy* signals the shift from utilitarian, basic functionality to a more luxurious future for the cruising houseboat: three-berth cabin, workshop, enamel stove, hot-water system and even a bath. To the nineteenth-century bargee, Rolt's vessel would have seemed as luxurious as a palace. Before the 1930s, of course, bathrooms were a rarity on board any type of houseboat, but the fact that by 1939 obtaining a bath specifically designed for a floating life was a relatively simple affair is a clear indication that houseboats were catching up with the sophistication of 'normal life' on land. Rolt reserves his hugest regret, of course, for the decline in work on the canals. The 'Number Ones' – that is, the boatmen who owned their own vessels and were essentially self-employed – were becoming few and far between. He meets several still working the Coventry Canal, one known as 'Four-Boat Joe', as they steer their four horse-drawn barges laden with coal between Atherstone and Oxford.

The Oxford Canal, where L.T.C. Rolt moored in 1939. Once a major industrial artery, the canal now boasts a thriving houseboat community.

He also mourns the physical decay of some of the waterways he was cruising in 1939. The Upper Avon Navigation, for example, he found in ruin – in fact, it had been decaying since the late nineteenth century. All the locks on this part of the river were derelict, and the course was dotted with abandoned mills, remnants of a vanished age. Clever Hill Mill had become a tea house, but others such as Harvington Mill lay gutted and rotting, the old mill-race was buried under thickets of overgrown reeds. On the Stratford Canal he came across an old man mowing grass near the Cut. Asking him when he last saw a barge pass this way, the old man pauses and replies ''bout four years back'. The gaffer explains that the railway company killed the canal for, as its owner, all the steam-train owners had to do was raise the waterway tolls to impossible levels, and all trade switched to rail. It was a common tactic. Bargees found themselves more and more plying their way along waterways owned by their enemies. It was a dying game. While in Europe many canals were being widened and modernised, in the UK, primarily because the railway companies owned most of them, many of the waterways remain as they have been since the eighteenth and nineteenth centuries.

On the Leicester Cut of the Grand Union Canal, in a 29-mile journey from Norton Junction to Market Harborough, Rolt does not meet a single other boat, and this on a waterway that was once a throbbing artery of the coal trade from the Midlands to the south. Braunston was of course still busy, with its long, straight village street alongside the canal, its marine shops and pubs, but the Braunston Tunnel, some 2,042 yd long, now offered no tug to the barges as a tow-through, having been withdrawn in 1935 owing to the decline of horse-drawn barges. Animal-towed vessels, though few and far between now, must have recourse to a friendly motor-boat to get them through.

Stopping at Long Buckby, Rolt is pleased to find the old canal shop still open on the wharf, whose painted watering cans have been sold to narrowboaters since the nineteenth century, and are still an essential item for every barge from Lancaster to Limehouse.

Long Buckby, and its adjacent hamlet Buckby Wharf, was once one of the busiest reaches of the canal, with wool and footwear and agricultural produce being carried to all corners of the land. The period 1900–45

By the time of Rolt's journey in the late 1930s many canals had fallen into decay. The once mighty Kymer's Canal, South Wales, choked beyond recognition.

saw a slow decline in the town's fortunes, but thankfully the early-nine-teenth-century bridge is now – as of 2020 – Grade II listed, as is the old Canal Shop, Anchor Cottage Crafts, still purveying its brightly painted metalwork to every houseboater who passes through. Back in 1939 the old man selling Rolt his wares waxed mournfully of the changes he'd seen in waterways life over the decades. With the challenge from road freight and rail, he explains, bargees have had to resort to fly-boating, the non-stop carriage of goods on a smaller, faster boat, seven days a week, twenty-four hours a day. He rues the day road freight overtook them, remembering the times when bargees were 'steady fellows, and tied up of a Sunday'. Despite the decline, Rolt did witness and record the vestiges of waterways traders – diesel barges now, of course, a Grand Union boat southward-bound with a cargo of coal; a pair of Fellows Mortons heading north, carrying 50 tons of sugar from Tate and Lyle in the Pool of London. Fly-boats all, making the 136-mile journey in fifty-seven hours.

Llangorse Lake, Breconshire, home to Iron Age water dwellers.

The Roman villa at Bignor, Sussex, supplying grain to traders on the River Arun.

The Thames western barge, ancestor of the narrowboat: with its flat bottom and single square rig, it was said to be able to 'go wherever a duck goes'.

The Aire & Calder Navigation, completed 1704.

Cremorne Gardens, Chelsea Embankment, by Phoebus Levin, 1864. Pleasure gardens proliferated in the eighteenth and nineteenth centuries, attracting weekenders and holidaymakers who
moored houseboats alongside.

Above left: All that remains of Cremorne Gardens today: the iron gates. It is a quiet yet pleasant
little park overlooking the Thames.

Above right: Kenneth Graham's immortal Ratty and Mole raised 'messing about on the river' to a
fine art in *The Wind in the Willows*, 1908. (Arthur Rackham)

The *Vital Spark*, one of the last of the steam-powered Clyde puffers. Unlike the horse, steam barges never tired so could travel the inland waterways and coastal waters non-stop. (Phil Sangwell)

Though picturesque, the River Brent at Hanwell, with its seven arduous locks, was the bane of all boating families. (P.G. Champion)

Sundowner, the private residential yacht owned by Charles Lightoller, rescued 130 soldiers at Dunkirk. (Stavros1)

Houseboats at Brentford, once the mighty hub of British inland waterways trade.

The canal at Yiewsley, home of the ancestors of Rolling Stone Ronnie Wood. (Justin Otto)

The River Deben estuary at Woodbridge, Suffolk, once a major inland port and still a thriving boat-building centre and water-dwelling community.

Matrix Island, a 130ft former Thames sailing barge moored at Wapping, at £3.5 million is Britain's most expensive houseboat.

Each of the houseboats at Shoreham reflect the owner's character.

Shoreham-by-Sea, West Sussex, home to a riverbank community in the estuary of the River Adur, where houseboat living and artistic expression are one.

Rolt passed through Long Buckby on the Grand Union: here pensioner Jim Pritty sits on a lock-beam. Jim was a boatman in the days of horse-drawn boats, and when Rolt made his journey, Jim spent his days preparing the locks for boatmen who were short-handed, for a shilling a time.

Rolt's classic work *Narrow Boat* is a book, then, that looks both backwards and forwards: back to the clearly fading world of the working barge but forward to … what? The author is in no doubt that in his hymn to life on the waterways he is celebrating more than mere leisure; he is giving an almost votive offering to a way of life that must be preserved lest we lose something deep, rich and valuable. He is at pains to defend his championing of canal life not simply as a reactionary, 'back-to-nature' philosophy but as a vital, living principle, that of maintaining a contact with a sense of place, with local materials, and craftsmanship. Writing in 1939, his was not a breezily optimistic conclusion – indeed, Rolt fears that the destiny of many houseboats of the future is to 'rot at the wharves'. But thankfully he lived to see a better outcome, for it was his pioneering salvoes in defence of the canals that led to the establishment of the Inland Waterways Association, the restoration of many neglected cuts, and the unfolding of a new destiny for those once-pulsating arteries of Britain – the post-war age of the non-working houseboat.

And what of river trade during the half-century 1900–45? Its story is much like the story of the canals; for while national and international trade itself boomed, its carriage by way of the Thames, Severn and Trent declined as the highway assumed hegemony over all things waterborne. The years between 1900 and 1945 saw an extraordinary expansion of the London docks, yet was a concomitant period of decline for the river bargee and his family. In 1909 the Port of London Authority was formed to oversee the extraordinary ongoing growth of the capital's docks: West India Dock, Millwall Dock and Albert Dock were all expanded, and by 1913 London was handling 20 million tons of cargo each year. By 1930 the city's port and docks employed no fewer than an astonishing 30,000 people. The River at Brentford was a bustling hive of industry, as we have seen in A.P. Herbert's novel *The Water Gipsies*; Battersea, Wandsworth and Fulham were forests of factories and mills. As for Britain's third great river, the Trent, its history as a trade route, while buoyed by the transport of petroleum in the early part of the twentieth century, experienced the same difficulties as the canals, with much trade seeping away to the roads. In H.G. Wells' *Tono Bungay* of 1909, he gives us a record of a journey on the Thames from Hammersmith to Blackfriars, marking the 'muddy suburb and muddy meadows' of Battersea and Fulham, and the coal barges wending their way on the tidal reach. While the timber trade along the Thames from Marlow in Buckinghamshire lingered on until the mid-century, the establishment of a railway station in 1873 signalled the end of water-trade as a populous profession. Marlow's story was replicated in river towns all over the country: where once a goodly proportion of the population would have lived on the river, now they were absorbed in other occupations – brewing, light industry, agriculture, road freight. This fate was suffered by Marlow's Oxfordshire neighbour, Henley, whose mighty reputation as a centre for river trade and bargees had lasted from medieval times. Once again the Great Western Railway became the mortal enemy of the river dweller, and in Henley from the late nineteenth century onwards, rebuilding of the waterfront transformed its character, turning it from a largely commercial area of wharfs and warehouses to one dominated by boathouses, villas and a hotel.

The twentieth century saw the decline of the classic Thames Sailing Barge, whose ochre-coloured sails had been a familiar sight for centuries. Working the Kent and Essex coasts and as far afield as the north of England, the South Coast, the Bristol Channel and – in the case of the larger seaworthy vessels, to continental European ports – these incredibly adaptable craft were capable of navigating the tricky sandbanks, shallows and eddies of the estuary with their cargoes of bricks, cement, hay, rubbish, sand, coal, grain and gunpowder. Timber, bricks and hay were stacked on the deck, while cement and grain was carried loose in the hold. They could sail low in the water, even with their gunwales beneath the surface. Clay and bricks from Essex, coal from Newcastle, hay and grain from Kent – these classic river and coastal barges were still in their heyday at the end of the nineteenth century when writer Joseph Conrad – himself a sailor – described the vista of the estuary at Gravesend from the prow of his ship *Nellie*:

> in the luminous space the tanned sails of the barges drifting up with
> the tide seemed to stand still in red clusters of canvas sharply peaked,
> with gleams of varnished sprits.

A classic Thames sailing barge at Wapping, 1884. Once a familiar sight on Britain's waters, by 1945 it was in severe decline.

But the well-metalled road did for the Thames barge as it ultimately did for the canals. While 2,000 barges were on the registry in 1900, these numbers gradually diminished. The last Thames barge to trade entirely under sail was the *Cambria* in 1970, the last freight being 100 tons of cattle cake from Tilbury Docks to Ipswich in October of that year.

We have seen that it was at the trading hubs of the waterways network that the first small communities of 'houseboat' dwellers began to form: Brentford, Braunston, Oxford, Denham, parts of the Regent's Canal, and of course the dull, wide expanses of estuaries such as Benfleet, Essex and Gravesend: it is in these places that the motley floating villages started to appear. The reasons for this pattern were obvious: when the majority of boats on the canals and rivers were working vessels, these locations were the places where a boatman and his family could obtain water, supplies and fuel. Here was a social life of sorts, with inns on the banks, where the shops of the village or locale were geared to marine necessities like rope, tea and foodstuffs. In short, where once a canal or river hub was a place to pass through quickly as a trader up against the clock, now it slowly became a fixed point of habitation for the twentieth-century houseboat dweller, and in so doing gradually became a more serene place where the clamour and cries of the warehousemen and lightermen of A.P. Herbert's Brentford in 1930 faded to become the sedate discourse and relaxed lifestyle of the occupants of Eel Pie Island and other quiet reaches of the Thames. In the early twentieth century at Iffley, Oxfordshire, houseboats were a familiar sight on the river as they wended their way, drawn by horses, by Nuneham Park. Who was living on them? Holidaymakers at first, for sure, but gradually the holidays lengthened to become a permanent cruising life.

In London, certainly, little houseboat communities had established themselves for decades, if not centuries, albeit informally: Drunken Dock in Millwall, which as early as the sixteenth century was an inlet on the south-east bank of the Isle of Dogs, was a public dock, used by anyone for mooring boats and barges, though it was also used for timber storage, with the permission of the Thames Conservators. In the nineteenth century willows grew along the banks and animals could graze down to the water's edge. Here many boatmen and their families put down roots, living there on a semi-permanent basis. Essentially, wherever river banks or tidal basins or inlets were unregistered land, there was an opportunity for houseboaters to moor.

No one in Britain could escape the war, of course, and the boat dwellers of the rivers and canals were no exception. From the very first strike of the clock at 11 a.m., 3 September 1939, and after the very first air raid, houseboaters had a special involvement. The Port of London Authority immediately established the River Emergency Service, a veritable aquatic army, wholly based on the waterways. Pleasure boats, steam launches and other large houseboats were requisitioned by the War Office to serve as large floating hospitals. The thinking behind it was that as the air raids destroyed infrastructure and hospitals on land, these waterborne medical establishments could take up the load, with hundreds of doctors and nurses up and down the river living and sleeping aboard what were effectively huge floating houseboats – not to mention the patients. Moreover, while enemy bombings put roads and highways out of action, rivers – despite being prime targets throughout the war for obvious reasons of their docks and ports – were never rendered useless by attack. However many bombs were dropped into the Thames, the Clyde or the Severn, the waterways remained open for freight and the movement of cargo and arms.

One might say that the Second World War was the British houseboat's finest hour. Never before in history had civilian vessels been recruited to join a military effort so huge that the defence of the entire nation depended on it. London, of course, was a particular target: the first significant attack came on 7 September 1940 when 375 enemy planes struck at the Thames and its docks. For fifty-seven consecutive nights the tideway was under almost continuous attack, with transport, communications, sheds and ware-houses destroyed or damaged. Bargees up and down the Thames became firewatchers, salvagers and rescuers.

A.P. Herbert, of course – the eminent barrister, author and resident of Britain's most famous houseboat *The Water Gypsy* – immediately took a prominent role in the River Emergency Service, supervising the tugs and launches that acted as a rescue force up and down the Thames. Untouched by debris or fire, the rivers of England became once again the main high-ways of the land, and although trade and shipping by 1941 was reduced to about one quarter of its peacetime volume, the waterways became essential for the feeding of the nation.

Elsie Waters was born in London in 1920 and became a Girl Guide then a Sea Ranger. When war broke out she was billeted on the *Marchioness* moored near Cheyne Walk, Chelsea and as a semaphore officer would signal to fire boat crew on the other side of the river. Rescue boats full of stretchers would ferry patients across the Thames to St Thomas's Hospital. Fellow officer Ruth Durrant remembers:

> At the time of the Munich crisis in 1938 I volunteered for the River Emergency Service ... they considered that London might be so severely blitzed it would not be possible to evacuate casualties by rail or road. So they had the bright idea of using the Thames pleasure steamers to get people out by water.

Ruth was stationed on the *Cliveden* at Cherry Garden Pier and recalls that the River Emergency Service contained a broad mixture of personnel from many backgrounds: Lady Violet Powell, daughter of the Fifth Earl of Longford and wife of Anthony Powell was a Voluntary Aid Detachment (VAD).

And it wasn't just river folk who were absorbed into the war effort, it was the canals too. With many boatmen called up, the Ministry of War Transport set up a corps of volunteer women to help work the family narrowboats. Sonia Rolt, the wife of waterways pioneer and author L.T.C. Rolt, joined up, and along with other volunteers was trained by Kitty Gayford to work a pair of boats – motor and butty – for the Grand Union Canal Company Southalls, operating out of Bulls Bridge in Hayes. As with the Land Army, this 'Canal Army' was the first opportunity for women from a non-waterways background to experience life afloat. In the extraordinary disruption that the war effected, one positive outcome was this broadening of horizons, a dissolving of boundaries between what one was expected to do in life and what one could now do. Many of the women, of course, returned to 'normal' life when the war ended, but many did not, including Sonia Rolt who spent the rest of her life on the canals.

It was mainly coal that the women of the Canal Army carried, along the Grand Union, Oxford and Coventry Canals, based at Hawkesbury Junction on the Coventry, a centre for the transfer of coal cargoes for the south. The life of the boating families at Hawkesbury during the war and beyond was the subject of a remarkable series of photographs by Robert Longden, whose work was compiled by Sonia Rolt in her wonderful work *A Canal People* (Sutton, 1997).

Dunkirk, rightly remembered as one of the nation's finest hours, must surely go down in history as also one of the shining achievements of the houseboat. For the mighty flotilla of 'Little Ships' that crossed the Channel from Ramsgate on that fateful day on 26 May 1940 consisted of the greatest armada of liveaboards ever seen. With one caveat – a lot of the boats were not crewed by their owners, but by naval officers and ratings. But many were, most famously, *Sundowner*, a motor yacht owned by Charles Lightoller, former second officer of the *Titanic*.

With men fighting at the front, women were drafted in to sustain the canal trade. Here flour is unloaded from the 'Heather Bell' at Tipton.

The recruitment of 850 'houseboats' as an impromptu armada was, of course, spurred by the unique shallow draft of these barges, pleasure yachts and steam launches. With hundreds of thousands of British and allied troops cut off by the Germans, troop ships were unable to get close enough for rescue. The only alternative was to utilise the private houseboats of the Thames and the south and east coasts – barges, launches and yachts. The Ministry of Shipping telephoned hundreds of boatyards from Hull to Southampton and ordered them to bring their vessels to Dover and Ramsgate as a matter of urgency. Thirteen Thames sailing barges were seconded, six of them built by R. & W. Paul Ltd of Harwich, Essex. A boat-building company with a long and fine tradition, R. W. Paul had been transporting malt and grain to and fro from Suffolk to London since the nineteenth century, some of their boats even seeing service in the First World War, shipping supplies across channel. Now, in another hour of need, the broad flat-bottomed barge – descendant of those first Roman vessels that navigated the perilous shallows of the Thames nearly 2,000 years earlier – came into its own.

A total of 850 'houseboats' crossed the channel between 26 May and 4 June, a motley flotilla of steam launches, fishing vessels, pleasure yachts, barges, rescuing 336,000 men. Operation Dynamo is replete with personal adventures: the lifeboat *Prudential* negotiated the 50-mile passage from Ramsgate to Dunkirk with eight small Thames work boats, known as wherries, in tow. These river- and canal-going vessels would be used to ferry troops from the beach at Dunkirk to the lifeboat. Many houseboats served thus: transporting troops, many of whom had stood shoulder deep in freezing water for hours, to the ships anchored further off-shore.

The 43ft-long *Marsayru*, her steel hull painted white with a blue fringe, fittings in brass, cockpit clad in mahogany, with a maximum speed of 9 knots, was another such triumphant houseboat of that glorious venture. Strafed by machine-gun fire from Messerschmitts, the *Marsayru*, captained by Gerard 'Dickie' Olivier – brother to the famous actor Laurence Olivier – nevertheless is credited as rescuing 400 soldiers. Today, above the boat's wheel, sits a small brass plaque that begins to tell her remarkable history. It reads, simply, 'Dunkirk, 1940'.

The motor yacht *Sundowner* was requisitioned by the Admiralty on 30 May. Its owner Charles Lightoller – the highest-ranking officer to survive the *Titanic* disaster – insisted that if anyone was going to take her to Dunkirk, it would be him and his eldest son, Roger, together with Sea Scout Gerald Ashcroft. The three men transported 127 soldiers back to Ramsgate, reportedly packed together like sardines, almost capsizing when they reached the shore. Now a museum ship at the Ramsgate Maritime Museum, *Sundowner* is one of many of the 'Little Ships' armada still celebrated today – indeed, seven of the actual flotilla were used in the 2017 film *Dunkirk*.

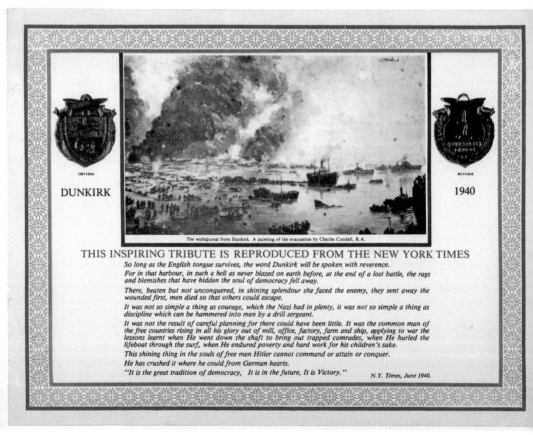

Approximately 850 'Little Ships' – barges, houseboats, steam launches and fishing vessels – took part in the rescue at Dunkirk. (Archives New Zealand)

Ex-D-Day
Landing Craft
at Cheyne
Walk, Chelsea
– heroes of
Normandy,
and post-war
houseboats.

If Dunkirk was the finest hour of the British houseboat, it had a near-equal almost exactly four years later when small boats were similarly dragooned into assisting the D-Day landings. For the final assault that began the liberation of Europe, vessels of all shapes and sizes began marshalling in London on 27 May. Never before had the Thames seen such a fleet of armed merchantmen and ships of war. On 6 June the D-Day armada set sail with 307 ships from London, carrying some 50,000 servicemen, nearly 80,000 tons of military supplies and about 9,000 vehicles. As the signal was given for the departure it must have been an extraordinary sight to witness the steady flow of deep-sea ships, coasters, tugs, barges, oilers and landing craft joined in the estuary.

And across the channel, as the soldiers neared the beaches of Normandy crammed into their Landing-Craft Assaults, or in the case of US troops the famous Higgins Boat, rifles poised, none of them could have known that in a matter of years many of these broad, deep vessels with their armour-plated mahogany hulls were to become miraculously transformed into the new fashionable houseboats of the post-war era.

As the street parties and the victory parades broke out across the country on 8 May 1945, an uncertain future lay ahead for the working barge, that stalwart of the rivers and canals for more than a thousand years. Society had been dislocated, turned upside-down by five years of conflict.

A new era was dawning, for both the country and for the houseboat.

5

ℭℭ AN ALTERNATIVE ℭℭ
SOCIETY

1945–2020

| LIVING AFLOAT AS A LIFESTYLE CHOICE IN POST-WAR BRITAIN |
| TRANSITION OF WORKING MARINAS TO RESIDENTIAL COMMUNITIES |
| NATIONALISATION OF THE CANALS | THE PLACE OF THE HOUSEBOAT IN CULTURE |
| NOVELS, FILMS *THE HORSE'S MOUTH, THE BARGEE, THE NAKED TRUTH, HANCOCK'S HALF HOUR* |
| THE HOUSEBOAT IN FICTION | PENELOPE FITZGERALD'S NOVEL *OFFSHORE* |

When in 1948 11-year-old Sally Bennett trudged back from the communal tap at Canvey to her 70ft converted barge *The Windmill*, moored on Benfleet Creek, with its living room, kitchen and two bedrooms, no electricity (all artificial light provided by Tilley lamps) and its small primus stove for cooking, the youngster could not have known that she represented a whole new generation of boat dwellers. A generation that neither worked on the river or waterway in trade, nor in an ancillary industry, but who worked (or went to school) on land, only through either choice or necessity living afloat.

Benfleet Creek is a peaceful offshoot of the Thames Estuary, surrounded by grey mudflats and pockmarked with inlets and eddies. A high street of shops runs parallel to the shoreline, a small bridge links the creek to Canvey, and factories and workshops thrive within walking or railway distance. For centuries Thames sailing barges and coastal boats had carried coal, grain and other goods from here to and fro up the east coast. Now, the war over, that trade was gone, and clusters of old vessels waited on the banks, still grouped around the now quieter trading hub as if in expectation of a return of an industry that never came.

The year 1945 brought a new government, a new spirit, and with it a sense of change. A spirit of confidence was in the air, of possibility, an optimism that was in a few short years expressed in the national celebration of the arts and industry, the Festival of Britain. But with victory had also come profound dislocation. Many thousands had lost their homes, and despite a growth in council-house building after the war there was an acute housing shortage leading to a proliferation of people seeking cheaper forms of accommodation away from the land. All these factors spurred the growth of little houseboat communities up and down Britain.

And what of the canals in this post-war era? A certain melancholy hovers over the last decades of the working waterways: though freight was still being carried right up to the 1960s, the tonnage was cut right back until gradually the only recipients were waterside industries to which road access was difficult – coal to the jam factories of Southall, aggregates shifting to and fro between Denham and West Drayton. The ship canals of the north still operated but when the entire canal network was nationalised in 1948

Houseboats at Chelsea Reach: the author aboard 'Moby Dick'.

the system was reshaped and categorised, the waterways divided into three: those that would continue to take traffic, those for cruising use and those that would be abandoned and left to rot.

Two government acts chipped away at the travelling houseboater's way of life: the 1944 Education Act, which laid down the minimum number of hours a child had to be taught in school, meaning that long trips on board for youngsters became untenable. A huge hostel for boating mothers and children was built at Erdington in Birmingham, but gradually families drifted ashore to permanent cottages and council accommodation. It was the end of the itinerant way of life for the working boatman and his family. The other transformative piece of legislation was the Clean Air Act of 1956, a noble and well-intentioned – not to say vital – law aimed at improving the health of the nation but which had the negative effect of drastically reducing the demand for coal as factories moved over to electricity and natural gas. Coal had been one of the biggest staples of water trade for centuries, so this was a decisive blow.

It was not that the actual life afloat itself had lost its allure. Many families persisted, but the carrying companies of old, some of which had started in early Victorian times – Samuel Barlow, Fellows Morton & Clayton – were now all nationalised, their liveries repainted with the yellow and blue of British Waterways, and at each trading post on the canal, instead of being greeted by a company representative, bargees would be confronted with the officialdom of a government clerk.

Some working boats turned to leisure, in a similar way to farms becoming petting zoos or cafes today. At Tooley's boatyard in Banbury, coal barges began to be converted into hotels: the *Mabel*, a 60ft carrier, was one day working for Atkins Ltd carrying house coal to Banbury and a short while later was reborn as a hotel, as was her companion butty *Forget-me-Not*, and the narrow boats *Nancy* and *Nelson*. Soon the canals were jostling with visitor trips, the *Halifax* and the *Warwick* becoming known for their pleasure cruises from Market Harborough to Foxton locks in the 1950s.

Thus the canal folk adapted. The change was slow but inexorable, but the worst effects of the transition were ameliorated by the formation in 1946 of the Inland Waterways Association, whose pioneering work publicising and arranging restoration of the navigable waterways that had fallen into disuse was a lifesaver for future generations, and smoothed the way for the canals to become one of the major new territories of a new form of houseboat living, that of the permanent but non-working 'cruiser'.

This metamorphosis was captured exquisitely in the Ealing film of 1945, *Painted Boats*, a drama–documentary beautifully directed by Charles Crichton that chronicles life on the man-made waterways at this pivotal moment in its history. With fictional canal families played by actors, yet real canal folk assisting in all aspects of production, the film presents a unique glimpse of life on the Cut as England moved from war to peacetime. The recurring themes of boat life pop up in the film – the isolation of the life, the lack of education, the rivalry between families who clung stubbornly to horse-towing and those who'd 'upgraded' to the motor barge. 'God made horses, but he didn't make motors!' protests Mr Stoner, captain of the *Sunny Valley* carrying coal along the Grand Union. 'Aye, and God didn't make my varicose veins!' retorts Mrs Stoner, after a particularly gruelling bout of legging. Like Rolt's *Narrow Boat* of six years earlier, *Painted Boats* is a eulogy, a paean to the canal families of old, clinging to a way of life that was ebbing away as fast as the new motorways were being constructed on land just over the green hedgerows lining the Cut. At one lyrical moment in the film the narrator Louis MacNeice recites a litany of these families' names: the Skinners, the Wenlocks, the Buckleys, the Beechams, the Stoners, redoubtable hardy stock still plying their trade between Langley and the Midlands. Yet these families are aware of the tug of destiny, and that their way of life is under threat. When Ted suggests to his sweetheart Mary that they abandon the water and live in a house Mary's response is one of horror: 'Live in a *house? Always* in one place?' She waxes lyrical about houseboat living, dreaming of them having their own boat one day where they can 'travel every turn of the canals, from Leicester to Limehouse, where the Cut joins the sea'. Won over, Ted plights his troth to Mary in the famous Boat Inn at Stoke Bruerne that has served canal folk since 1877 and is still run by the same Woodward family to this day. Her father, Mr Smith, is holding out against the mechanisation of his horse boat, and deeply resents the motor vessels that do nothing but 'churn up the water and knock down the bank!' Yet he too is forced to succumb to the inevitable and is ordered by his company to have a motor fitted at Nurses Boatyard at Braunston. *Painted Boats* is shot through with a special pleading for the continuation of canal life, emphasising that 'coal does not go bad, coal can go by water' and despite the motorisation of the boats, there is an underlying melancholy acceptance that while working boats have their place in British industrial life, it is a diminishing one.

As mentioned in the previous chapter, the first houseboat communities began to blossom around former trading hubs – Brentford, Braunston, Oxford, Stoke Bruerne, Denham – and around the smaller wharves of London such as Chelsea Reach. Some mushroomed in estuaries, heirs to the trading centres that had flourished in the golden days of river transport.

Benfleet sits in a relatively sheltered creek that is an offshoot of the estuary in Essex, and became home to one such notable 'floating river village'

The once mighty Bridgwater canal. By the 1970s there was scarcely any trade or industry on the waterways. (Chris Denny)

of the post-war era, its boats made up of a motley collection of old working barges from the nineteenth century, contemporary converted landing craft, and Thames sailing barges.

Helen Bootle remembers her grandfather owning *Hearts of Oak* in the 1930s, a 45-ton working barge built in 1879, which in the immediate post-war period became a houseboat on the Essex marshes and the home of the Andrews family. Nick Ardley was brought up on an active sailing barge, the *May Flower*, built in 1888. Many houseboat communities expanded after the war but residential boats existed in Benfleet Creek during the conflict and earlier. Terry Hutchings remembers his father, Reg, living aboard *Le Hope* in the 1940s:

> I was born in 1949. The family (then) lived in Walthamstow and we would go down for weekends. When, in 1963, we moved to Benfleet for a couple of years all that remained of *Le Hope* was the rectangular bottom of the barge surrounded by the sea of dune grass that covered what had been the creek.

Sally Bennett lived in South Benfleet from 1948 to 1955. They moved to a houseboat, *Blue Peter,* on the creek to be nearer to Canvey railway station so her father, a soldier, could travel to Woolwich every day. With no electricity or running water, Sally vividly describes life aboard the boats. Water had to be carried from a communal tap near Canvey Bridge, a Tilley lamp (paraffin) was used for light, and a primus stove for cooking. Rainwater was collected in a cistern, and there was a small parcel of land for washing lines and flowers. As with most houseboat communities on the Thames, the tide would come in twice a day and Sally recalls the gravy on their plates sloshing about from side to side as they ate.

Interspersed with delightful memories of being closer to nature – picking blackberries and mushrooms on the downs – houseboat life was also prey to the darker side of the natural world, including the wrath of storms. Most notorious was the Great Flood of 1953: on the night of 31 January a tidal surge came down the North Sea, flooding low-lying lands in its path. Canvey Island was badly hit, its sea wall washing away in the Tewkes Creek area. Fifty-eight people lost their lives and the island was evacuated.

Nearby Benfleet was not unscathed. Some boats were destroyed, including *Blue Peter*, Sally Bennett's boat:

We lived temporarily on the *Windmill* until we bought the *Millie*, which was situated much closer to the Canvey bridge. As an 11 year old, I was able to carry back from the tap two 2-gallon containers of water. Both the *Blue Peter* and the *Millie* were converted barges about 70 feet long, I think. Each had a living room, a kitchen two bedrooms and a toilet. For heat we had a little freestanding coal-burning fireplace; I remember it had two little doors with mica windows.

The houseboat community at Benfleet was hardy, industrious and innovative. As Jacqueline Newman remembers:

A houseboat at Benfleet Creek, one of the first post-war 'floating villages'. (Benfleet & District Historical Society)

I and my family lived on the houseboat *Veronica* in Church Creek. It was a converted landing craft and my Dad built a room on the top deck for my two brothers to sleep in as we were a family of seven. We lived on it for about seven years from 1946.

These landing craft were now ubiquitous as houseboats. With their large steel encased hulls and their depth, and their potential for expansion and conversion, floors or decks could be added, and with their broader beam than narrow boats they offered greater living space, and the look and feel of a cottage.

It's clear from the memories of those who lived on the boats at Benfleet that their jobs were varied: soldiers, shopkeepers and in the case of Michael Reed's Aunt employment at the nearby Glanfields Clothing Factory. This was the new generation of houseboat dwellers, who made their living not from the rivers or canals on which they lived but from land-based employment.

Like Benfleet, Chelsea Reach on the tidal Thames near Battersea Bridge started life centuries ago as a working wharf, for coal barges and sailing barges. In 1860 it comprised Lindsey Wharf and Greaves Boat Builders, operated by brothers Walter and Henry. As a main offloading point for cargo to the western reaches of the capital, the busy nature of the riverside always contrasted with the quiet residential stretch of roadway that became Cheyne Walk. Greaves was not only a boat-building yard but also a Thames ferry service, with boats to let. Chelsea Reach also possesses a rich cultural heritage. The painter Turner lived at 118 Cheyne Walk, and American artist James MacNeill Whistler frequented the boatyard to work on his majestic impressionistic depictions of the Thames, being first a customer and gradually a friend and inspiration to Walter Greaves, who himself became an accomplished artist.

It is precisely a heritage such as this that led to many spots on the waterways like Chelsea Reach becoming liveaboard villages in the post-war era. Chelsea Yacht & Boat Company actually began life in 1935 as shipwrights and marine engineers, carrying out dry-docking refits, overhauls and repairs. By 1942, the employees at the company had increased from half a dozen to over one hundred. At the end of the war, Landing Craft and Motor Torpedo Boats arrived back at the boatyard and along with numerous sailing barges, became houseboats. Still flourishing today, the Chelsea Yacht & Boat Co. is the oldest working boatyard in London.

It is this mixture of converted sailing barges and landing craft that gives Chelsea Reach its particular motley character, perhaps lacking in some of the canal communities which for obvious reasons consist mostly of narrow boats. Each houseboat moored in Cheyne Walk is distinct, having evolved over the decades since the 1930s as successive owners have added to them.

The perception of boat dwelling as being somehow 'countercultural' was firmly part of the zeitgeist of the 1950s and '60s. When comedy has to have its finger on the pulse of the nation's funny bone, it is telling that in an episode of the very popular sitcom *Hancock's Half Hour* – 'The Poetry Society', it is a group of bohemian folk who live on barges that are the butt of many of the jokes. Hancock has invited his new artsy friends round to 23 Railway Cuttings, much to the chagrin of his cynical friend Sid James. 'My friends and I rebelling against conformity,' announces Hancock grandly, adding, 'We are the avant-garde of the new culture.' He explains that none of them have houses. 'Haven't got houses? Where do they live?' queries a baffled Sid. 'Well ten of them live on a barge on the canal,' is Hancock's reply. He outlines the occupations of these proto-hippy liveaboards:

> Well, during the day we pursue our various artistic sidelines. Some of us make pots and jugs, and then there's Adelaide – she's very good on the raffia mats. Then there's Percy and his Welsh bedspreads. Some of us paint, and sculpt, and the rest of us lie in bed, thinking.

Clearly a dig at bohemian houseboat life, and a caricature, but the central core must have contained some truth for it to resonate with an audience, that those choosing to live afloat in the 1950s were motivated – if only in part – by a desire to reject mainstream society. In the film *The Naked Truth*, 1957, it is not artists but those of a slightly shady criminal bent who live on the water. Dennis Price plays the crooked editor of the eponymous grubby expose magazine who blackmails celebrities and politicians. His home on the houseboats at Chelsea Reach conveys the film-maker's desire to portray the floating village as somehow existing on the margins of mainstream society, a fraternity of outsiders just as likely to commit crime as create a work of art.

The following year, 1958, it was a return to the houseboat dweller as artist in *The Horse's Mouth*, again filmed in and around the marina on

Cheyne Walk, where the painter Gulley Jimson lives, played with gruff and magnificent eccentricity by Alec Guinness. Jimson lives and works aboard his boat and is part of a motley gang of artistic outsiders who inhabit the fringes of Chelsea society, in constant conflict with local wealthier residents and the forces of officialdom in the shape of the council. *The Horse's Mouth* is a portrait of the houseboat-dweller-as-outsider par excellence, as a rebellious Jimson chooses to demolish his own artwork – a church mural – before it can be destroyed by the mandarins. In bitter triumph, he sets off downriver in his barge, shaking a fist at the London that has rejected him.

Houseboats as the domiciles of communist spies is territory trodden by the taught thriller *The Deadly Affair*, made in 1966 and once again filmed around the very photogenic Lots Road, Cremorne Gardens and Cheyne Walk riverside. A gritty, dour adaptation of the John Le Carre novel, Maximilian Schell plays Dieter Frey, a psychopathic cold war agent who, like Gulley Jimson and Dennis Price before him, has chosen to hole himself in one of the houseboats in Chelsea Reach. This much sought-after

Chelsea Reach in 1860. Many houseboat communities were descendants of working wharves dating back centuries.

location was yet again immortalised in the Tom Courtney film *Otley* of 1968, a man-on-the-run picaresque that sees the eponymous Courtney hide out in the colourful barges and landing crafts of SW10.

Perhaps the most comprehensive elegy to canal life in films is Galton and Simpson's comedy film *The Bargee*, 1964, starring Harry H. Corbett of *Steptoe & Son* fame. The central comic conceit is that, like a sailor with a girl in every port, Corbett has a sweetheart at every canal stop along the Grand Union, from Rickmansworth to Leicester. A satire of the new officialdom that had beset the waterways since their nationalisation, with government clerks overseeing the bargees' every move like foremen in a factory, *The Bargee* paints a picture of the post-war liveaboard as one whose way of life is being squeezed on all fronts, from the decline in traffic and precariousness of work to the oppressiveness of the new bureaucracy he is forced to contend with. Once again the perennial theme of whether a 'landlubber' can ever truly embrace a life afloat is painted in the relationship between Hemel Pike (Corbett) and one of his sweethearts, Christine the lock-keeper's daughter, played by Julia Foster. Once they are betrothed, Corbett tries his best to adapt to working on land and fails miserably, while his new bride – at first reluctant to live on a barge – presents him on their wedding day with a newly painted working boat along with a butty. The canals are due to close in twelve months' time, and all freight cease, but the newly married couple launch their vessel with gusto for a final year on the Cut.

Perhaps the most substantial and vivid portrait of houseboat living in fiction in this period is *Offshore*, the novel by Penelope Fitzgerald. Published in 1979, it depicts her life from 1961–63 aboard the converted sailing barge *Grace* moored on the Chelsea embankment. In a brutally honest account, *Offshore* depicts a community neither of the river nor the land, a gallery of finely drawn misfits whose motives for living afloat, while varied, are characterised by a certain dysfunctionality. This is no idealisation or romanticising of boat life. While appreciating the beauty and singularity of their surroundings on a stretch of the river that was, indeed, sought out by the artist Whistler, Fitzgerald is not shy to paint a picture of hardship, instability and angst amongst the motley community of outsiders who maintain a precarious hold on life in the hidden, mud-caked world of the tidal Thames. In the book, the houseboats are

Above: The famous Bulls Bridge Junction on the Grand Union, one of the locations for the 1963 Galton & Simpson film *The Bargee.*

Left: The houseboat in literature: Penelope Fitzgerald's *Offshore* is a bitingly realistic account of her life aboard the barge *Grace,* moored at Chelsea Reach.

described as being on Battersea Reach (now called Chelsea Reach), a mixture of old sailing barges, converted landing craft, and even a mine-sweeper. As detailed above, the Chelsea Yacht Company (still extant) is descended from the old boat yards of centuries past, including the long reign of Victorian boat builders Greaves & Sons, and today is a community of prosperous owners and renters conscious that they live in a highly desirable part of the capital. In the time Fitzgerald is writing of (which incidentally is the same time as the author was growing up on the boats – our home, *Moby Dick*, was only a few vessels down from *Grace*) the community was a magnet for transients. In *Offshore* the boats are occupied by an ex-Naval officer, a male prostitute, a middle-aged marine artist, and sundry small families either rocked by semi-separation or having 'fallen' from a former prosperity. An air of shabby gentility hovers over the floating village. A group of nurses from the Waterloo Hospital rent a barge at the end of the line and are told off for playing loud music. A police launch remonstrates with them – this is the early 1960s and record players were a part of every young household, floating or otherwise – but the police end up making friends with the nurses and giving them regular lifts to work on their launch.

Fiction, of course, yet Fitzgerald's book perhaps provides a necessary counterbalance to the somewhat romantic depictions of boat life in A.P. Herbert's *Water Gipsies* of three decades earlier. The physical reality of the environment – that is, living on the river but not working on the river – is more than merely a metaphor for a hybrid existence but a concrete truth. The owners of houseboats have to maintain their boats in exactly the same way as the old sailor and bargees would, hoisting them up in dry dock every couple of years, maintaining a constant regimen of ongoing repairs, yet without the actual everyday benefit of their vessel being a working boat. All these houseboats are like retired old folk – Fitzgerald's barge, *Grace*, was built in 1907. For several of the characters in the novel the need for regular maintenance is almost overwhelming. In a particularly poignant scene, Willis the marine artist is so euphoric he has finally sold his boat *Dreadnought* that he throws a small party in the deck house, only to find that the small leak in the hold has ruptured, resulting in the barge sinking right in the middle of the celebrations.

Life, in short, was no bed of roses for houseboat dwellers in the 1960s, even in Chelsea, for though London SW10 was, and is, a salubrious part of the capital, it rubbed shoulders with a district of deprivation and neglect. Lots Road, leading to Sands End, Fulham, was an area of dark-brick working-class terraces loomed over by factory and brewery chimneys. And the boats were part of that shabbier, neglected district; part of it, yet not quite belonging to it. So, too, the people, wanting to be inhabitants of Chelsea yet not fully possessing either the desire or the capabilities to live fully in their midst. Tourist cruisers at the time would pass under Battersea Bridge and the guide would bellow through his megaphone, 'And on your right, ladies and gentlemen, the *artistic* colony of Chelsea' – at once delineating its distinctness from the land-based population, for even though it was certainly not the case that all the occupants of the boats were artists (nurses, clerks, ex-naval personnel, and more are noted in Fitzgerald's novel) the perception lingered from the 1950s that anyone who chose to live aboard a barge or a converted landing craft must *ipso facto* be a bohemian.

Offshore is a somewhat melancholy depiction of houseboat life, but nevertheless is a valuable corrective to the romantic view that living afloat affords an untrammelled life of freedom from worry, routine and drudgery. For anyone who has experienced it, that is patently not the case. Being closer to nature offers a nourishing kinship with seasons, wildlife, the ebb and flow of the natural ways of the tide, but on the flipside, a proximity to nature can also mean being forced to confront dark, negative forces, not least hostile weather, decay, brutal cold, storms and disaster.

I myself grew up on the *Moby Dick* at Chelsea, a converted landing craft that had served at Normandy, which with its robust steel hull with mahogany lining was a warmer and more secure home than the large and often draughty barges. The child's experience of houseboat living is, of course, very different from the adult's, imbued as it is with none of the work and all of the fun. For me, living on the boats at Cheyne Walk was a wild, windy world of footloose recreation: days of playing in the grey Thames mud below the huge snakes of chains that lashed the vessels to the slimy walls as thick as a castle's; the postman regularly hosing us down from the single tap at the standpipe; the vast riverscape - the Thames is particularly wide just upstream of Battersea Bridge, and though daunting was never frightening, lacking as it did the restless temper of the sea. There was disturbance, however, in the form of the weather. Unprotected by the narrowness of streets and the barriers of buildings, the boats were prey to unfettered wind and rain that would come slamming down the estuary to collide with the craft, making them jostle together like animals seeking comfort in a herd. The result of one particular storm was the gangplanks being blown away, and our pathway to the shore was temporarily gone. We were cut off for a day, like islanders marooned, destined to watch the people and the cars on the embankment going about their daily lives without a care in the world while we sat trapped on our vessels, staring. This, I think, was the only time I felt the separation of us boat dwellers from human life on land. It was not acute, but it struck me as being something that clearly set us apart. Our reliance on one narrow length of wooden walkway to connect us to the rest of society was brought home to me, and made me aware of a certain vulnerability in our way of life.

There was another time when our boat – unmotorised, unlike some of the other houseboats – broke free of its moorings in the middle of the night like some rebellious pet, and unknown to us sleeping aboard floated silently and darkly out into the middle of the Thames while we snored. My father recalled waking in the morning light to unfamiliar sounds – no faint traffic noises from the early commuters on Cheyne Walk, no seagulls picking at the flotsam and jetsam by the big grey walls, only a kind of dull quiet and a mild lapping that filled him with foreboding. He emerged on deck to see a wide, glittering river in place of the comforting chain and embankment wall. One by one we gathered aft and stood, blinking, in the morning sunshine, seeing a view we'd never seen before: the Chelsea Flour Mills and the cigar-like chimneys of Lots Road power station, the red buses crossing Battersea Bridge and the pointing pedestrians on the Surrey side, waving to us and shouting, as though we didn't know we were in the middle of the river.

Towed back by a friendly tug, the danger passed, if danger there was, and life resumed: a life of wandering the Chelsea of the early 1960s. Mick Jagger was pointed out to me, at that time living with his fledgling band The Rolling Stones in a terraced house at the Lots Road end of the embankment; Augustus John the painter, and the colourful delights of the Kings Road – Antiquarius, the Cafe Picasso, the eye-popping mercantile pleasures

The author aboard *Moby Dick*, which was sold to the Bloomsbury writer Edward Garnett.
Houseboat living by then was a choice of many artists and bohemians.

of Peter Jones Department Store, and the exciting red-brick rebelliousness of the Royal Court Theatre in Sloane Square, which at that time was stirring up London with the work of Harold Pinter and John Osborne.

Stefanie Harwood, 87, has been a resident at Chelsea Reach since 1964, renting a converted wooden-hulled infantry landing craft, *Mudlark,* until 1967, when she designed the *Mallard,* built by the Chelsea Yacht and Boat Company. At that time a second line of houseboats was being built at Cheyne Walk, and pontoons were being added. With their flat hulls and extremely shallow drafts – a mere 8 inches – pontoons had many advantages over the large but ageing Thames Sailing Barges, many of which were falling into a condition that rendered them beyond repair. On a broad pontoon the options for larger accommodation – wide living rooms, bars, spare bedrooms – were greater than the smaller landing craft and contributed to the shift of boat dwelling from one of moderate hardship to considerable luxury.

These then were the houseboaters of the new era: motley, drawn from all classes, some falling, others rising; eccentric some, others orthodox. My parents sold the *Moby Dick* to the writer Edward Garnett of Bloomsbury Group fame, and we moved ashore.

Another major houseboat community lies in Braunston, Northamptonshire. As we have seen, the marina was originally developed at the turn of the nineteenth century as the waterways depot at the northern end of the Grand Junction where it joined up with the Oxford Canal. Several original buildings from the Georgian and early Victorian periods are still in their intended use, and the marina's entrance itself is dominated by the dramatic cast-iron bridge dating from 1834, erected by Thomas Telford. Since the decline of trade on the canals, the metamorphosis of Braunston from industrial centre to liveaboard village has been complete. Now a major centre for leisure craft and narrowboats with modern mooring facilities for 250 boats, plus a large, busy brokerage selling all types of new and used steel narrowboats, Braunston is a huge success story of reinvention. With dry and wet docks, craneage pad and a service area capable of most repairs, a bargee from Victorian times – whilst being struck by the modernity of the technology – would nevertheless recognise the same crowded Braunston he sailed through in the 1800s with his cargo of coal, salt, wine, ale, china or fancy goods.

Brentford marina on the Thames opposite Kew is perhaps one of the locations most illustrative of the post-war transition from trade to residence. As we have seen, for more than a century Brentford Dock was a major hub and focal point between the Port of London, the canal system and the Great Western Railway. In 1964 the barges unloaded their last cargo, the dock was closed as a shipping point and the site disposed of by the British Railways Board to the Greater London Council. Plans were drawn up by Sir Roger Waters in 1968 and the area rebuilt as a mooring marina and waterside housing development. It now boasts a sixty-berth marina for boat owners in West London looking for leisure mooring on the Thames, with access to the canal network as well as the upper reaches of the non-tidal Thames. With laundry, water and electricity, wi-fi and nearby supermarket, it is a far cry from the coal-dust-filled caterwauling mayhem that A.P. Herbert experienced in the 1920s when he steered his barge *The Water Gipsy* north to the Grand Union. Gone are the vast brick warehouses, the cranes and the smokestacks: the area now is replete with an air of peace and gentility. Floral gardens and walkways border the waterways, and an artistic community thrives on 'Johnson's Island' on the Grand Union, once home to the old station master's and lock-keeper's offices, and at one time part of Brunel's original Brentford Dock; now home to sixteen art studios, surrounded by dappling canal views and colourful narrowboats.

Brentford is by no means the largest mooring marina for cruising houseboats – Whilton near Daventry has berths for 200. Marinas festoon the Oxford Canal, one of the oldest in England, and from Braunston to the Thames a houseboater can find pocket communities of travellers with bankside facilities for every need. Nick Corble, author of *A Beginner's Guide to Living on the Waterways* (The History Press, 2017), bought his narrowboat in 1999, living in Oxford for half the year and the other half in a house in Bucks. Woodbridge in Suffolk, Bulls Bridge in Hounslow, Denham in Buckinghamshire as the Grand Union meets the Chilterns – numerous aquatic villages now pockmark the nation, often hidden away from the gaze of the land dweller.

Cruising the waterways has become a popular pursuit of both the obscure and the famous. Renowned acting couple Timothy West and Prunella Scales are famous travelling houseboaters, spending many years travelling the inland waterways in their narrow boat. 'Perhaps with a child-hood like mine,' writes Timothy West in his book *Our Great Canal Journeys*, 'a disposition to itchy feet is understandable.' Their numerous voyages are chronicled in the book, and in their long-running TV series, including a notable trip journeying London's 'lost route to the sea' south from the Thames on the River Wey, then a connecting hop by road to the Arun, which, as has been seen in earlier chapters, meanders south through Sussex to Littlehampton, a waterway used for trade by the Romans. It was inspired by the journey of J.B. Dashwood in 1867, whose book *The Thames to the Solent by Canal and Sea, Or the Log of the Una-Boat* Caprice, recorded his navigation of the then complete route (the Wey & Arun Canal having been built in 1816). Lack of freight led to its abandonment in 1871, and it fell into disrepair, although 23 miles of it have been restored since 1970, with the aim of returning the link to its former glory, but the Wests had to effect a 10-mile transfer by motor car to complete the journey.

It is no mere coincidence that actors have long been drawn to houseboat living. From Elizabethan times touring has been the staple of the working actor, and the nomadic affinity between boating and the thespian life is strong. Commissioning a new build from Tooley's, Banbury's famous boat builders, the Wests launched their 60ft narrowboat in 1988 and have been enthusiastic part-time nomads ever since. 'We had no idea, at the time, how many happy memories from our lives would come to pass on our precious boat,' wrote Timothy West in his love letter to the waterways, *Our Great Canal Journeys*. The actress Susan Penhaligon is another famous thespian who has made the river her home.

As life on the working canals ended relatively recently, a matter of fifty years or more, there are countless people alive today who are first- or second-generation land dwellers whose parents and grandparents were bargees. A famous figure connected by blood to the waterways is Ronnie Wood of *The Rolling Stones*, whose life represents in microcosm what happened to the working boat people of Britain. Wood hails from a long line of navigators and helmsman with a family lineage dating back to the 1700s, and he is one of the first of his family to be born on dry land. Ronnie himself affectionately refers to his ancestors as 'water gypsies', both his parents, Elizabeth and Arthur, being born on canal barges, the *Orient* and the

Antelope. They were employed by a contractor, Sabey & Company, moving cargo up and down the canals between Manchester, Stratford-upon-Avon and London, and like many bargees, during the war Ronnie's father was not permitted to enlist, as working the canal barges moving vital cargo around the country was considered too important for the nation's survival. Once the war was over Wood's parents settled down on dry land in Yiewsley, Middlesex; near enough to the Grand Union Canal for his father to keep in touch with his bargee friends and take Ronnie fishing and messing around with the boats.

From 1945 to the present, then, in addition to the permanent liveaboards, there has grown up a vast swathe of the house-boating population that can be described as temporary cruisers – those who choose to spend weeks, or even months, on board travelling the inland waterways network but whose principal domicile is on solid ground. This kind of houseboater has proliferated in recent years, almost to the point at which the canal system, which between its phase as an industrial network and its current status as a locale for, almost exclusively, recreation and escape, was, as Liz McIvor describes it, 'ribbons of calm' (*Canals, The Making of a Nation*, BBC Books, 2015). The ribbons of calm were not to last long. The phrase 'victim of its own success' is a cliche, yet can be applied, with caution, to the Inland Waterways Association, which since 1946 has, with no hyperbole, rescued the canal network for the nation. Yet by dint of its very success it has created problems of overpopulation. Many boats now compete for moorings, and space is diminishing, particularly at those parts of the country where a confluence of traffic has the potential to cause as many delays as the M6.

So, with the story of the British houseboat brought up to the present, what of its future?

6

⁋❨❩⁊ A NEW LIFE ❨❩

THE PRESENT

| CURRENT STATUS OF HOUSEBOAT LIVING |
| RENAISSANCE AS A RESULT OF ECONOMIC PRESSURES ON THE HOUSING MARKET |
| THREATS TO THE WAY OF LIFE | NEW DESIGNS AND ODD DESIGNS | THE FUTURE |

Houseboat living in Britain has perhaps never been more attractive as a way of life, yet its situation is uncertain. With tenures less stable than those of houseowners, houseboaters have in recent years (at the time of writing, 2020) been subjected to litigious actions that threaten the very future of living afloat. The community at Chelsea Reach in London is involved in an ongoing legal case that has gone to the High Court and the Appeal Court: the subject is complex but concerns the owners of the Chelsea Yacht and Boat Company issuing new agreements that stipulate more dry-dock maintenance than the boat dwellers were previously obligated to perform, an insistence that is perceived as an attempt to evict some of the older boats and install super-yachts of the very rich. Needless to say this would permanently alter the character of this ramshackle floating village in London SW10, disfiguring a community that has grown up over the last eighty years. Waterman's Park in Teddington is likewise existing beneath a shadow cast by those powers that be, that wish to develop the bankside at the expense of the floating residents.

Similarly, canal life, especially in the cities, is changing. As pressures on the housing market continue following the 2008 financial crash, more and more people have been seeking accommodation on the water, and as that demand has increased there has been a consequent rising of mooring fees. In the capital this has become a particular challenge for boat owners, who are beginning to see their environment changing from a relatively economical choice to a way of life just as expensive as on land. In 2020, 250 London boat owners received a letter from the Canal & River Trust, the charity that manages British waterways, notifying them of mooring fee increases of up to 89 per cent. Many feel the new fees will be unmanageable. Joseph Caldwell, 47, is being asked to pay £12,000 a year in mooring fees for his berth in central London. 'I've been living on my narrowboat for fourteen years,' says Caldwell:

> My mooring used to have a vibrant community. Now more and more people are being forced to abandon their homes and neighbours, and the place is turning into a leisure pied-à-terre for rich people that is half empty all the time.

This phenomenon of the houseboat as a luxury second home is not new. We saw in Victorian times the growth of the weekend pleasure-boater like the artist Walter Dunlop and his London friends. The wealthy professionals today who own holiday vessels moored on the Thames or the canal system are simply heirs to those who have across the centuries used our waterways as places of pleasure and relaxation, but today it is more ubiquitous than ever. It would certainly have amused and possibly amazed the hard-working bargees of the Victorian age to know that the Cut that was for them an environment of hard, grinding labour is now a place of ease, peace and recreation.

This change in the demographic of houseboat owners is having an impact on the nature of the floating settlements; how much longer can they be perceived or described as 'bohemian' or 'different'? Certainly in many places the old camaraderie exists, the old instincts to travel and be free, to submit to the 'call of the wild', but more and more, one feels, the separation that has existed for centuries between those who dwell on land and those who live on water – a gulf that has formed a recurring leitmotif of this book – is waning. If you are a chartered accountant or a digital marketer working in Canary Wharf, London, and living on a 70ft yacht in Limehouse basin, you are not going to develop your own language and slang when on the water, or insist that your progeny only marry within the boating community. A 130ft converted sailing barge recently went on sale at St Katherine's Docks, London, for £3.5 million. With its five bedrooms, sauna, jacuzzi and jet-ski launch, it is a long way from its former life as a grubby haulier, wending its way up and down river with its bulky cargoes and its coal-caked skipper.

The shift of houseboat owning from bohemians to the super-rich is, of course, not the whole picture; boat dwelling can still give opportunities to many individuals and families seeking a life 'that little bit different' yet not financially challenging. While the cost of living afloat is not as low as many aspiring houseboat purchasers might envisage, owing to maintenance, mooring fees, consumables, etc., it's nevertheless a viable move, at least outside London. The truth of the matter is that the social and economic makeup of those living afloat probably reflects more or less the differences in ordinary land-based society.

Bob Golding and his family have lived on a wide-beam barge for five years, first at Priory Marina in Bedford and then at Whitemills, Northamptonshire, on a new self-designed vessel. For them, it was initially a financial decision – no mortgage, no excessive overheads – but it soon metamorphosed into a quality-of-life change, with the wildlife, the huge skies, the feeling of being closer to nature, being the chief rewards.

'I've seen hundreds of species of all types of creature, whatever the season. It's the ultimate calming tonic to start your day to,' says Bob:

> The winters are cosy; multi-fuel (eco approved) is both romantic and cockle warming, but we also have central heating. No council tax, minimal fuel costs, cheap mooring fees, we save nearly £2,500 a month from when we were living in a house in St Albans previously by living on a boat.

And what of the houseboat community Bob and his family have encountered?

> Marina and river communities are just fantastic in our experience. We seem to all have each other's back and if there's a problem with your boat then the chances are someone else has had the same problem and knows how to sort it. Our marina is small so we all know to respect each other and help each other when needed. We love it.

Priory Marina Bedford, with its combination of static floating homes and moorings for cruising houseboats, is a typical state-of-art example of the future of life afloat. (BWML, Aquavista Marinas)

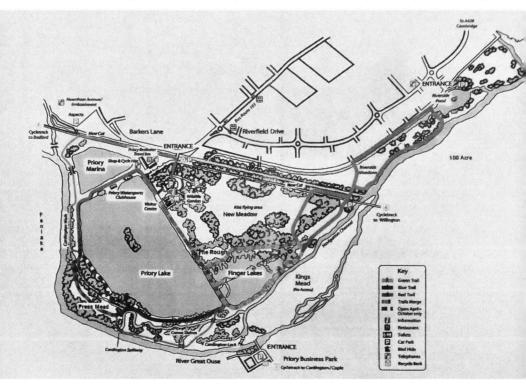

There's quite a cross-section of people on boats. From people on a low budget to early retired couples who spent their house-sale profits on an all-singing all-dancing boat, and everything in between. Lots of creative people, makers, artists, musicians...

And contemporary life on board a houseboat is not without its dramas: 'drinkers falling in the canal, the odd tragic suicide, occasional swan-flights causing accidental injury, water-pipes freezing over.' In Bob's experience rivers are less safe than canals, and the occasional sight of rescue boats – 'thankfully rare' – can make for a dramatic atmosphere.

Purpose-built houseboats are of course not a new phenomenon, but many are the result of conversions and ad-hoc extensions such as the post-war landing craft or the expanded sailing barge. For some decades now many narrowboat builders have been designing and building craft for a residential not working life. From Uxbridge to Ellesmere Port and everywhere in between there are boatyards working away at fulfilling the growing demand for a floating life. And for non-moving houseboats, of course, the potential for ambitious design is almost unlimited.

Perhaps one of the most 'freestyle' and unlimited examples of house-boat communities – and one that is hopefully surviving the pressures of bureaucracy and the 'powers that be' – is Riverbank, Shoreham-on-Sea, West Sussex, on the estuary of the River Adur. As with other floating villages around the country, Riverbank began in the 1920s as a motley settlement of ex-sailing bargees and coastal boaters whose lives, literally, ran aground when trade declined. Like Benfleet and Chelsea it is a mixture of D-Day landing craft, converted barges and even a German torpedo boat – now a four-bedroomed home. All vessels are sublime expressions of the owners' individualities, but none more so than the houseboats belonging to extraordinary artist and boat-designer Hamish McKenzie, who has augmented his seven houseboats – the community numbers fifty – with such found materials as tractor wheels for windows, rusty ambulances as deck rooms, and even the nose cone of a Jumbo Jet as the prow.

Hamish McKenzie is almost a perfect crystallisation of what a house-boater has been and perhaps always will be: one who has not quite 'fitted in' to the norms of society, or chosen not to, and who has embraced living on the edge, literally, as a mode of being. Like his namesake, Compton Mackenzie's fictional 1950s artist Gully Jimson, Hamish has made designing houseboats his art and his life, and in so doing proves that the British houseboat is more than merely a species of accommodation but an emotional and perhaps spiritual way of life.

We have traced the story of aquatic life on the inland waterways of Britain from the first tribes who ventured along the great rivers for purposes of trade or simple curiosity, through to the dynamic Romans who built the first canals, to the bargees who for 2,000 years steered their floating homes along the Ouse and the Thames and the Severn, laden with cargo, then along the dozens of man-made cuts that criss-crossed the first industrialised nation on earth, when floating homes were the blood cells coursing through the veins of the body politic. We have marked the unique character of these aquatic folk, with their distinct language, music and art, detailed the toughness of the life, the dangers, and acknowledged the strength of spirit required in order to meet such a life.

And we have reached the twenty-first century. Though the shape, look, feel and cost of a houseboat may have changed, the impulse to take to the water, to feel the 'call of the wild', to lead a life on the edge, on the fringes and hinterlands of human society, is the same as it has always been.

SELECT
ᴥᴥ BIBLIOGRAPHY ᴥᴥ

This book is principally the fruits of fieldwork augmented by the rich quantity of river and canal literature. Below is just some of the essential reading for those interested in pursuing further the topics and themes covered:

Ackroyd, Peter, *Thames: Sacred River* (Chatto & Windus, 2007)

Babbs, Helen, *Adrift: A Secret Life of London's Waterways* (Icon Books Ltd, 2016)

Burton, Anthony, *The Canal Pioneers: Canal construction from 2,500 BC to the Early 20th Century* (Pen & Sword, 2017)

De Salis, Henry Randolph, *Bradshaw's Canals and Navigable Rivers of England & Wales* (Blacklock & Co., 1918)

Emerson, Peter, *Wild Life on a Tidal Water: The Adventures of a House-Boat and her Crew* (Samson Low, 1890)

Fagan, Dick and Burgess, Eric, *Men of the Tideway* (Robert Hale, 1966)

Haughey, Fiona M., *People and Water: A Study of the Relationship Between Humans and Rivers in the Mesolithic and Neolithic with Particular Reference to that Within the Thames Basin* (University College London, 2009)

Hanson, Harry, *The Canal Boatmen 1760–1914* (Manchester University Press, 1975)

Herbert, A.P., *Water Gipsies* (Methuen, 1934)

Higden, Ranulph, *Polychronicon* (1300s)

Hollingshead, John, *On the Canal: A Narrative of a Voyage from London to Birmingham* (The Waterways Museum, 1858)

Jones, Tony, *The Liveaboard Guide* (Adlard Coles, 2019)

Leslie, George Dunlop, *Our River* (Bradbury, Agnew & Co., 1888)

McIvor, Liz, *Canals: The Making of a Nation* (BBC Books, 2015)

Mackay, Dr Charles, *The Thames and its Tributaries* (The British Library, 2010)

McKee, Eric, *Working Boats of Britain* (Conway, 1983)

Pearse, Mark Guy, *Rob Rat* (T. Woolmer, 1878)

Pratt, Derek, *Waterways Past & Present* (Adlard Coles, 2015)

Rolt, L.T.C., *The Inland Waterways of England* (Allen and Unwin, 1950)

Rolt, L.T.C., *Navigable Waterways* (Penguin, 1985)

Rolt, L.T.C., *Narrow Boat* (The History Press, 2014)

Rolt, Sonia, *A Canal People: The Photographs of Robert Longden* (Sutton Publishing, 1997)

Smith, George, *Our Canal Population* (EP Publishing 1974)

Thacker, Fred, *The Thames Highway* (David & Charles, 1968)

The Diary of G.R. Bird, Wharfinger, Boat-Builder and Carrier, 1820–30 (unpublished, held at Birmingham Reference Library)

Thurston, E. Temple, *The Flower of Gloucester* (Williams and Norgate, 1911)

Walford, Edward, *Old & New London* (Cassell and Company, 1891)

West, Timothy & Scales, Prunella, *Our Great Canal Journeys* (John Blake, 2017)

Wigglesworth, Neil, *The Social History of English Rowing* (Routledge, 1992)

Wilkes, Sue, *Tracing Your Canal Ancestors* (Pen & Sword, 2011)

Wilkinson, Tim, *Hold on a Minute* (Allen & Unwin, 1965)

✣ ACKNOWLEDGEMENTS ✣

During the writing of this book I have consulted with many people who currently live on the waterways: I thank in particular Stefanie Harwood at Chelsea Reach, Bob Golding, Hamish McKenzie in Shoreham, and Susan Penhaligon on the Thames at Teddington. In addition I thank the staff of the London Canal Museum, Ellesmere Port Inland Waterways Museum, Hull Museum, Dover Museum, Stoke Bruerne Canal Museum and the Ramsgate Maritime Museum, in addition to the staff at the many marinas I have visited up and down the river and canal network. I would also like to thank Amy Rigg and Alex Waite at The History Press, and Samuel West for the Foreword.

✣ ILLUSTRATIONS ✣

All illustrations are either sourced from the public domain or original photographs taken by the author. I would like to thank the curators and staff of the museums for permission to photograph some of the historic maritime artifacts and boats in their collections, and for the staff at marinas for permission to photograph some of the boats moored at their sites.

INDEX